6/17 3-26 UDS/17
14/19

D0392734

BORN TO
BLOG

Building Your Blog for
Personal and Business Success
One Post at a Time

WITHDRAWN
FROM
COLLECTION

MARK W. SCHAEFER
AND STANFORD A. SMITH

New York   Chicago   San Francisco   Lisbon   London   Madrid   Mexico City
Milan   New Delhi   San Juan   Seoul   Singapore   Sydney   Toronto

Copyright © 2013 by Mark W. Schaefer and Stanford A. Smith. All rights reserved. Printed in the United States of America. Except as permitted under the United States Copyright Act of 1976, no part of this publication may be reproduced or distributed in any form or by any means, or stored in a data base or retrieval system, without prior written permission of the publisher.

1 2 3 4 5 6 7 8 9 0   DOC/DOC   1 8 7 6 5 4 3

ISBN: 978-0-07-181116-3
MHID: 0-07-181116-8

e-ISBN: 978-0-07-181117-0
e-MHID: 0-07-181117-6

This publication is designed to provide accurate and authoritative information in regard to the subject matter covered. It is sold with the understanding that neither the author nor the publisher is engaged in rendering legal, accounting, or other professional service. If legal advice or other expert assistance is required, the services of a competent professional person should be sought.
>   —From a Declaration of Principles Jointly Adopted by a Committee of the
>   American Bar Association and a Committee of Publishers and Associations

McGraw-Hill books are available at special quantity discounts to use as premiums and sales promotions, or for use in corporate training programs. To contact a representative, please e-mail us at bulksales@mcgraw-hill.com.

This book is printed on acid-free paper.

Contents

Introduction:
Were You Born to Blog?

W e love to blog.

In fact, it is the best part of our jobs. And we've had some success—both of us have developed successful personal blogs that have led to new business connections, personal and business benefits, and yes, even new customers.

We've also built blogs for dozens of organizations from Fortune 500 giants to small retailers, schools, government agencies, and nonprofits.

Blogs are the content engine driving the social web. In addition to providing a unique voice of authority, they are undeniably critical to any digital marketing initiative. Even if nobody reads them, blogs are a powerful contributor to search engine optimization efforts, creating PR opportunities, and providing a platform in a time of crisis.

The many important and proven benefits of blogging led us to have many lively conversations around this one question: "Why do so many blogs suck . . . and what can we do about it?"

The idea for this book was born!

To let our personalities come through in this text (which will make it so much more interesting), we'll occasionally pause and tell individual stories to make a point. Let's start that now.

MARK: My blog *{grow}* was squarely in the "suck" category for nearly a year. I started it as an experiment. After all, if I was going to consult about marketing and teach it, I needed to immerse myself in the new media.

As a classically trained marketer, I started my blog with a well-defined marketing message that I wanted to deliver to my target audience of business prospects. It sounded good on paper.

Two things happened. First, nothing happened! I just got no traction at all and very few comments or engagement for months. Second, I became bored.

So instead of sticking to a script, I started to relax and just be myself and blog about whatever interested me. I told stories about my marketing journey and connected the dots between traditional marketing and social media. I challenged myself to try different styles. I let my funny side come through and experimented with video blogs.

Then, an amazing thing happened. Instead of me finding my target audience, my target audience found me! The blog started to grow and attract international attention. I was on to something, and this led me to reflect on the common themes of my success and the success of others. Was it possible for an individual, or a company, to be built to blog? What made the best blogs sing and hum with excitement?

STANFORD: I know the exact moment I became a Lady Gaga fan. It was June 29, 2010, the moment my post "Lady Gaga's 8-Point Guide to Larger than Life Blogging" was published.

I wrote the post as a way to cleverly (in my opinion) point out how the pop icon and social media maven could offer some advice to new bloggers. I had run across a *Rolling Stone* article about Lady Gaga and immediately saw a decent blog topic.

In my gut, I knew that I had a cool concept. Lady Gaga was in the news after flipping off Mets fans, and I figured I could get a few extra eyeballs by drafting behind the news story.

The post took a week to write since I chickened out at least three times, refusing to publish the post until I had exhausted every excuse. The mouse icon hovered over the "publish" button for a full 10 minutes before I quickly clicked the button, stood up, and walked away from my desk.

It's gone, I thought. *Can't do anything about it now.*

Back then I was scared of my own shadow. I still believed that only renowned writers like Malcolm Gladwell or Seth Godin had the right to publish.

After taking a walk around the block, I returned to my desk to start my ritual of begging and pleading for attention on the interwebs.

I had a list of about 25 blogging bigwigs that I had been stalking on Twitter and discussion forums. I used Twitter to send each a direct message asking them to take a look at my Lady Gaga post. Then I waited, watching TweetDeck for mentions of the post.

In 10 minutes, Brian Clark from Copyblogger, a top-10 online marketing powerhouse, linked to the post. Next Chris Guillebeau, bestselling author of *The Art of Non-Conformity*, sent the link to his Twitter followers. Marketing expert Jay Baer weighed in, too, flooding my site with a new surge of curious readers.

I was transfixed.

I kept refreshing the page to get an updated count of the number of people who had retweeted the post. Every refresh added a new retweet translating into thousands of new people seeing the post.

Within three hours more than 120 people had retweeted the post, resulting in almost a half million impressions. I had my first hit post. I thought that was the end of the run.

I was wrong.

Three weeks later, I spotted a forum message from Brian Clark with an invitation to write a guest post for *Copyblogger*. This was a real coup since *Copyblogger* was known for being extraordinarily stingy with guest post slots.

I also was selected as a Top 50 Netsetter by Jade Craven, a respected networker and blogging talent spotter. The listing led to *Pushing Social* getting included in several other award lists and attracted hundreds of visitors to my new blog.

One blog post was the starting gun for a string of opportunities that led to new friends, business contacts, and a platform to help thousands of bloggers.

But something kept poking at me. Slowly over two years I put words to the question that became an obsession: Could anybody successfully start and grow his or her own blog?

A year ago, I decided to see if there were more people like me. It didn't take me long to find them.

In fact, the web is packed with successful bloggers who are scared to death of blogging. They were as mystified by their success as I was. Puzzled, I read hundreds of "About Me" pages hunting for clues to their "accidental" success. I dissected an equal number of posts looking for their secret sauce—the magic that transformed them from shy scribblers into powerful and influential bloggers.

What we found surprised us. The bloggers we came to know and learned from all had common traits and applied a similar set of skills. Depending on the blog, they were *dreamers, storytellers, persuaders, curators,* or *teachers.* Some stuck with one dominant skill. Tim Mazurek, the publisher of *Lottie + Doof,* an award-winning food blog, is an engaging storyteller and uses his skill to bring his food recipes to life. Patricia Zapata from *A Little Hut* is a methodical and prolific curator of DIY crafting projects that are fun to make and eco-conscious too.

We realized that these skill sets aren't exclusive to bloggers. We all have them, to some degree. We all dream about our future, tell stories, persuade and advocate for what we believe in, curate information and objects that matter to us, and teach in formal and informal ways.

What connects us is the challenge of finding the right medium for expressing ourselves and sharing what we've learned and observed. While technology has offered paper, canvas, radio, and TV, it's only recently that we've had blogging as an elegant tool for expression and two-way dialogue.

Through blogs, we've gained the capability to express our thoughts while benefiting from the collective experience of readers. Along the way, we've discovered that blogging isn't just a publishing tool, it's a stage for our beliefs, values, and dreams. It's a place to establish our personal power and help our companies stand out. Millions are discovering that once they step on that stage, they begin a process that transforms lives.

YOU HAVE THE SKILLS YOU NEED

Many people think blogging is an all or nothing deal. Either you have a talent for blogging or you don't. This notion haunts us because it is wrong.

The goal of this book is to show you that anyone—with a little coaching—can blog. We'll go one step further and argue that you already possess most of the skills you need to be an extraordinary blogger.

Blogging is also a tool that any business can use. It is not reserved for deep-pocketed corporations. The *Born to Blog* approach can transform every employee into a talented blog contributor. Instead of looking for the perfect blog writer, businesses can focus their attention on empowering individuals through the enterprise.

How to Get the Most Out of *Born to Blog*

We begin *Born to Blog* by examining the essential traits and five blogging skills that everyone possesses to some degree. Each of these skills can become the foundation of an effective blog. We show you how to recognize your particular skill and ignite it for your life and business writing.

Next we present you with specific business tactics and approaches that naturally flow from your business's culture and unique value. We also explore how personal blogs can be used as a platform for turning hobbies into profitable businesses.

Then we examine the key characteristics of exceptional personal blogging. This will help you to identify and use your innate strengths to create and grow your own blog by examining the work of exceptional bloggers and their unique approach to creating blogs that matter.

Our Philosophy

Blogging and social media are a lightning rod for strong opinions and viewpoints. We know how easy it is to get distracted with "minor" details while missing the "major" principles. So we want to lay out our philosophy.

1. There Aren't Any Right Answers (Yet). There are many bumper-sticker sayings in social media that masquerade as truth. While some are helpful, such as "Be Human," others are so abstract that they are rendered useless: "Be Authentic."

We are not shooting for platitudes and are loath to contributing more buzzwords to the conversation. We are simply offering suggestions based on our observations and experiences. Experiment and use your own results to render an opinion on whether our points are right or wrong.

2. Respect Your Intuition. Blogs influence their writers in unique ways. Pay attention to your instincts and let them guide your actions. Our goal is to give you tools for sharpening your perspective and expression of your beliefs.

3. Relate, Don't Compare. There will always be a blog that is bigger and gets more readers or retweets than your own. Trust us—you don't want to get in a comparison game with other bloggers. Instead, find the similarities and lessons you can learn from other blogs, but stay focused on your unique strength. In the end, you'll protect your sanity and make quicker progress.

4. *Why* Before *How.* *Born to Blog* is an exploration of how blogging is changing people and businesses from the inside out. In the end, we believe that once you understand the connection, you will be able to use your blog in surprising new ways. It's easy to get sidetracked by technical details and blogging tactics. A quick search on "blogging" will deliver hundreds of millions of articles on the practice of blogging. While we could fill this book with this type of information, it wouldn't help you.

Instead we'll tackle the "inner game" of blogging first. We'll show you how to recognize the five core blogging skills you already possess and teach you how to put them to work for you and your business. Once you understand the spirit and mindset of exceptional blogging, you'll have the confidence and vision to implement blogging tactics.

So let's begin, with the help of a medical doctor who had a really, really lousy blog.

CHAPTER 1

The Common Traits of Successful Bloggers

I t got to the point that Raman Minhas hated his blog.

After four years of patient and consistent blogging about issues in his industry, biotech, Raman felt that he was spinning his wheels.

"I had built up a blog readership over that period of about 1,000 readers," the U.K.-based physician said. "And I was getting around 300 hits per month, but after all those years of blogging, I hit a wall. There was *no* organic growth of my readership, and no real reader feedback, no matter how hard I worked. After four years, I was disenchanted with blogging. Without any positive feedback, the blogging process became wearisome and I came to dread the 'time of the month' to write.

"Once in a while, I would read an inspirational blog post that would keep me going for a few more weeks, but I had to find a way to push through these blogging barriers or it simply could not last.

"So, I took a time-out," Raman said, "performed an internal review, and decided to refocus on a more interesting topic, medical technology. A subtle change, but I'd previously spent six years as an emergency room MD in the U.K. and was more comfortable with the technology side of the business than the abstract chemistry of new potential drugs.

"With a clarification of my niche, my focus became much clearer and I was reenergized. I found I could write more easily, and many more topics came to mind. Writing finally became enjoyable! Through the medtech theme, I was also able to connect to my interests in entrepreneurship and value investing. This was such a breakthrough. Slowly, the page hits began to grow—perhaps readers gauged more passion and a renewed sense of energy in my content? And the blog was starting to get NOTICED. I was invited to present at an industry networking event on the use of blogging in our industry. This was a small audience (around 60) but highly relevant. It was a milestone for me!

"Slowly I was finding my blogging 'voice,' and with this positive feedback, my confidence grew. I decided I needed to work on being more consistent and that I needed to grow my engaged network of readers. As my blogging changed, my audience changed too. I was now getting picked up by important medtech CEOs and investors. I decided that to grow the blog I needed to write at least weekly. This felt daunting.

"Here was another barrier I faced. Would I have the time to keep this up? Would I have enough to write about? I decided that I needed to make the time and this needed to be central to my business. My wife and I decided together that I was going to go for it, and I learned to make the time and started posting weekly, without much trouble, as it turned out.

"Consistency definitely helped. I could see the page views and readership grow! I also spent time systematically building my target audience on Twitter, using the advice in the book *The Tao of Twitter*. These people seemed to love my content. In a short period of time I tripled the number of page views on my blog, and it's still growing! I was energized!

"After all those years, my blog was finally starting to create some business victories:

- I was asked to attend an important two-day conference and moderate a panel on commercializing medtech. This is fantastic exposure for me and my business. Another breakthrough! To be authentically helpful, I am using my blog to give the conference exposure. I'm helping the organizers with sourcing medtech CEOs from my own network for other panels in the conference. It's a win-win-win for us all.
- One of my recent posts was picked up by an industry news organization, and it was put up on the front page of their website as a news item. This was incredible PR, and hits to my blog went up. It was so successful, they asked if my posts could be a regular feature on their site. Of course, I said yes.
- One of the CEOs from a high-profile company commented on one of my posts and subsequently introduced me to one his VC investors (a very influential group within my target audience).
- Another powerful CEO connected to me through my blog, and we are already discussing ways of working together. Things NEVER used to move this fast. It's as if the blog is a noninvasive, trust-building relationship booster.
- At an event in February this year, I met another powerful industry leader for just five minutes. But we have had the chance to continue to get to know each other through the comment section of my blog. The blog community is loyal to me and is helping me succeed.

"I have learned a lot along the way. Patiently and steadily build rapport and trust with your readers. Write about your passions. It takes time to find your blogging 'voice.' Authentic helpfulness and reciprocity go a long way. It wasn't easy, but today my blog is a fun and central part of my business."

Raman's story is not unusual—in fact, it's rather typical. There really are very few overnight successes in the blogging business. So let's dissect and explore some of the traits we learned from his experience.

TENACITY

Raman never gave up, even when he became disheartened. It takes time to find your voice, to connect with your audience, to learn how to appropriately build and promote your blog, and to write in a manner that connects with busy readers (more on that in the next chapter). Chris Brogan, one of the most successful marketing bloggers on the web, famously said it took him three years to earn his first 100 subscribers.

Using the ideas in this book will certainly lessen your learning curve and put a rocket behind your opportunities. But we can't teach you how to blog. You have to be committed, and you have to keep at it and learn by doing.

> **MARK:** I often get asked the key to blogging success. My instinctive answer is usually, "Work like hell!" In a society conditioned for instant gratification, blogging can better be described in terms of an athletic ability that only becomes stronger with sacrifice, practice, and patience.

TAKE ACTION

If you are starting or building a personal or company blog, you should be mentally prepared to keep at it for a couple of years to make it work. There are no shortcuts. You can't buy a blog following. Your community has to be built patiently, one person at a time. Raman involved his wife in his decision to keep at it. Like anything in life, blogging takes a commitment.

FOCUS ON YOUR PASSIONS

Raman's success flagged when he became disinterested in his original blog topic. By refocusing his energy on a topic that excited him, his passion and energy flowed through his words. Of course that is going to come through in his writing!

If you're not passionate about your subject matter, you're on a short road to failure. You need to focus on one general topic so your readers aren't confused, but you can certainly work in lots of other hobbies and ideas. Both of us are eclectic people who enjoy sports, history, travel, art, and the outdoors. Although we typically write about business subjects on our blogs, we bring in all of these passions to help tell our stories and make a point.

> **STANFORD:** Readers are drawn to passionate people. They feed off the blogger's intensity. When I first started writing, I adopted an all-business, "just the facts" approach to my posts. I studiously erased any emotional element that could dilute my logical arguments. These posts bombed. Slowly I realized that readers wanted to see how I felt about a subject. It was uncomfortable at first, but I began to open up and share my opinions and

sometimes intense perspective on certain subjects. To my surprise (and delight), my readers ate it up. My passion gave them permission to engage with me on an emotional level. I now believe that passion is the "secret sauce" for powerful blogging.

TAKE ACTION

How do you find that passion? Try this exercise. Write out the headlines of 30 different blog posts you would like to write. Don't worry about the content—just write the headlines. Now look over this list. What is the common theme? Is it gaming? Pets? Books? Relationships? Is the list aligned with your business goals? Do you need to have multiple blogs to cover multiple topics? Developing a list like this forces you to think about writing for the long haul.

FLEXIBILITY

Raman exhibited flexibility in a number of ways in this case study. First, he was willing to find his voice and change over time. When he was getting no traction, he stopped and adjusted his topic so it better reflected his true interests. It's not unusual to start down one direction and then end up someplace else!

Finally, Raman was keenly in tune with the needs of his readers. Comments and feedback were important to him. These reader connection points energized him and provided inspiration for blog post ideas.

TAKE ACTION

After six to nine months of blogging, conduct a simple self-audit by asking yourself these questions:

* What posts were the most fun to write? How do I write more like these?
* What posts received the most interaction or feedback? What did I learn from them?
* Am I still having fun writing about this topic? Do I need to broaden my scope, narrow my scope, or change altogether?

CONSISTENCY

Raman's big breakthrough came when he decided to blog every week instead of once a month. The reasons for that are simple.

If you think about some of the benefits of blogging we've discussed—search engine optimization, brand awareness, and customer connection—they can only come with consistency. One blog post per month won't do it. Your customers need to be looking forward to hearing from you on a regular schedule.

STANFORD: Om Malik, the founder of GigaOM, a leading tech blog, said that his blog's success came in part from his discipline of publishing daily. When I read this, I committed to publishing a new blog every weekday. Although the daily goal scared me, I felt that my readers would appreciate more content.

The first week was tough. The second week was easier, and by the fourth week I was easily publishing quality content on a daily basis. In fact, I discovered that writing every day was easier than once a week! I've spoken with other "daily" bloggers, and they agree that their schedule is easier to maintain than a weekly or monthly posting schedule.

MARK: One obstacle to consistency is an assumption that every blog post has to be profound. It doesn't have to be. In fact, short, simple observations and "how-to" posts often do the best!

TAKE ACTION

The idea of blogging creates a mental hurdle for many people. Let's reframe this. Can you write a 500-word essay once a month about something that is interesting to you? In analog terms, that's one page double-spaced. Sure you can so that! And if you can do that, you can blog!

Now, for a second post, write a summary of a particularly interesting article you read for work. Provide proper attribution, of course, and a link back to the original article. Add a short commentary of your own about why you liked the article. There's post number two for the month. That wasn't so hard, was it? You're on your way to being a consistent blogger!

COURAGE

Last, but certainly not least, is courage. That might seem strange to put in a book about blogging, but it is probably the single biggest obstacle on the road to blogging success.

It takes courage to put your ideas out there for the world to see.

It takes courage to be vulnerable, to even be wrong sometimes.

And yes, it takes *a lot* of courage to push that "publish" button.

MARK: One of the hardest lessons has been learning to open up with people and show a little bit of a personal side on the blog. And yet, whenever I do, I'm always rewarded for taking that risk.

I have written about 1,500 posts for my blog {grow} and other blogs, and there has not been a single one I have been completely happy with. But if you aim for perfection, you'll never publish anything. Having the courage to be good instead of perfect is a part of blogging success and the trade-off you have to make to be consistent.

TAKE ACTION

Yes, you can learn to be courageous if you have enough desire to succeed!

First, give yourself deadlines, and then publish whether you think the blog is perfect or not. For many people, especially those with perfectionist tendencies, you may never push "publish" if you wait for perfection!

Second, trust your audience. On average, out of every 1,000 comments on a blog, there might be one that is unkind. That's a pretty favorable ratio! In general, people on the web are very supportive. Eliminate the fear of criticism from your mind. It's probably not going to happen, and if it does, that means you have made somebody think. Job well done!

OK, there is one more trait we need to cover that is fairly universal. To be a great blogger, you have to be a great writer . . . or do you?

CHAPTER 2

You're Not a Writer, You're a Blogger

O bviously you need to have some writing competency to be a successful blogger. But blogging is much different from the type of writing you might have practiced in school, primarily because blog readers are so different.

Blog readers usually are mixing business and pleasure when they visit a blog. On the business side, they are often hunting for new information. They have a problem to solve, and they may have followed a result from a search engine and arrived at your site. Other times, another person they trust has linked to your site and they've arrived out of curiosity.

On the pleasure side, they have lowered their "corporate" guard because they assume that your blog is informal. They hope that you can deliver your information with wit, humor, or in an easygoing manner that is approachable and genuine.

However, as you would expect, there are some tried-and-true rules for writing interesting and compelling blog posts. Let's look at a few straightforward ways you can dramatically improve your blogging skills . . . with a little help from a jazz star!

FIND YOUR VOICE

You may never have heard of Ernie Watts, but he is among the greatest jazz saxophone players anywhere. If you're a fan of jazz, you can recognize his distinctive sax "voice" even if you were listening to a new recording.

Ernie has a live recording called "To The Point: Live at The Jazz Bakery," and in this recording, he explains the demands of distinctiveness and immediacy in music, but it also serves as a perfect description of a successful formula for blogging. Ernie says:

> *When you record live music . . . that's it . . . everything has led to this. All the practice, all the other gigs, everything you've ever done, comes down to today. This is as good as I get in this moment. Tomorrow is another matter. We'll get up again and practice and try to get a little better . . . but this music is about the point of truth today.*
>
> *It's about "Who are you?" and "What do you do?" You listen to [jazz great] Charlie Parker and you listen to John Coltrane and Thelonius Monk, and you have all that in your head, but it still gets down to who are you in relationship to all of this. Because no matter how hard I practice, I will never be John Coltrane. I'm me and I'm coming from where I'm coming from.*
>
> *So at a certain point in your life, you get to that. That's the point of truth, that's your point of reality. It's who you are.*

This quote sums up the imperative for originality in successful blogging so well. You may read other bloggers and admire other bloggers, but at the end of the day, it's about "Who are *you*?"—about how *you* fit in, *your* point of truth in this moment in time.

Like Ernie's sweet and unique sax tone, you have to find your own "voice" too. It is literally the only way to stand out in this overcrowded world we call the social web. We don't need repetition and sameness. We need *you*. We need your moment of truth.

> **MARK:** When I have people guest post on my blog *{grow}*, I challenge them to write a post that *only they could write*. It can be a difficult challenge, but this discipline always results in a more interesting story!

TAKE ACTION

When you write a blog post, always try to connect the subject matter to your unique experience, your story, and perspective. This can be particularly difficult if you are working in a buttoned-up corporate environment, yet many excellent blogs have found a way to bring a human, personal touch to the content by trusting employees to be honest and approachable.

Other unique characteristics to blog writing that can help you connect with your readers are described in the following sections.

BLOG UPSIDE DOWN

No, we don't mean standing on your head!

Most writers have been taught to write an article or tell a story in a linear fashion: a beginning, a middle, and an end. That usually does not work for blogs.

The problem is that people who read blogs are starved for time and are impatient. They are not going to wait until the end to get to the punch line. You have to give them the punch line first and *then* tell them who, what, when, where, and why. Turn your blog upside down!

In journalism school they used to call this "burying the lead"—making readers work for the main point of the story. Most blogs can be improved by wiping out the first third of the story. Have the courage to put your blog under the knife.

KEEP IT SHORT

Continuing on the "hurried blog reader" theme, shorter blog posts—under 1,000 words—seem to work best in most circumstances. We believe you have to earn the right to go long. The more credibility you have, the more time people will stay on your blog. If you are just beginning, new readers are going to give you just a few moments to make your case—if you're lucky. If you're Malcolm Gladwell, you can write 10,000 words without a care.

Respect your readers and their precious time. Get in, make your point, and get out.

HOIST A HEARTY HEADLINE

If you are a serious and experienced writer, this next piece of advice is going to be unpopular. Headlines are the most important part of a blog. Without a scintillating, compelling, tweetable headline, your hard work will never see the light of day.

People who read blogs scan headlines to determine if your precious work deserves to be read. As bloggers, we need to help them know to choose us.

Here's an example of a poor headline: "My biggest blogging challenge." Somebody set the alarm to wake me when it's over. It might be a *great* blog post, but the headline is just a snoozer. Plus it can't be easily tweeted. When you use the word *my*, it will look like it is the tweeter's biggest blogging challenge, not yours. So you have to keep "shareability" in mind!

Don't make headlines an afterthought . . . maybe you should even write the headline first!

HAVE THE COURAGE TO BE IMPERFECT

When you are creating a work for the world to see, it is frightening to be imperfect. Yet how can you be original *without* being imperfect? The best bloggers are real. Human. Less cautious than the average author. A role model for us in this respect is Gini Dietrich, of Chicago's Arment Dietrich agency, especially when she uses her video blogs to connect with readers in a highly personal way. Gini lets us know when she's stressed, disappointed, worried, mad—what is happening with her in the moment. There is awesome power in that authenticity.

DON'T JUST WRITE, REWRITE

People will spend more time with you if they enjoy your writing. Bloggers can't hit it out of the park every time, but when they do, it's probably because they found a way to make the words sing. Go over your writing and take out any words that don't move the story along. Look for new ways to add a clever phrase or a bit of humor. A helpful trick—read your post aloud to see if it has a natural, conversational tone.

ENTERTAIN ME

"Entertainment value" is not a phrase commonly used in business classes or journalism schools. Yet with the cacophony of voices vying for your attention, isn't entertainment paramount today? Think about the content you enjoy and share. It's likely that there is some element of entertainment involved.

Mix it up. Add video, photos, interviews, reviews, humor. Be surprising. Mark added Friday cartoons to his blog. Why? Because it is an element of fun that was not being offered by anybody else in the space.

Use creative visual elements, bring in other authors to spice up the conversation, blog about a provocative, open-ended question, write from a different perspective. Entertain!

Now you might find it odd that we haven't mentioned anything here about the actual subject you are writing about! Does it matter? If you create a post with (1) a captivating headline, (2) a unique personal view, (3) a personal risk, (4) an entertaining spin through (5) words that sing, won't that be a joy to read?

We'll cover more about the *what* of blogging later in the book. But first let's get back to those all-important common skills of the world's best bloggers!

CHAPTER 3

Yes—*You* Can Blog

Katie was fed up. For most of her life, Katie had fought a losing battle with obesity. A love affair with sweets and two pregnancies had added over 129 pounds to her small frame. The pounds, however, masked a fierce determination to change. Three years ago, Katie decided that she would lose the weight on her terms.

And she decided to share her struggle to lose weight with strangers.

She started her new blog, *Runs for Cookies*, on Google's popular free Blogger service. The goal was simple: deputize her readers in her war on obesity. The blog's name reflected her desire to have fun while losing weight. Running would burn calories while leaving enough wiggle room for her passion—cookies.

Katie knew that writing about her struggle with losing and keeping off the weight would keep her accountable. The blogging process would also help her examine her thinking, knowing that a poor mental attitude would show up in her blog posts.

Runs for Cookies quickly grew. Katie's willingness to share painful memories, private doubts, before-and-after photos, and plastic surgery details earned a devoted audience of fellow weight-loss warriors. Once Katie reached her weight-loss goal, the blog morphed into a "maintenance tool" to chronicle her struggle to keep off the pounds.

Bit by bit, the shy and private stay-at-mom grew into a savvy storyteller.

Some would think that Katie had an advantage that made her weight-loss battle and blog a success. They would be wrong.

Katie isn't a multi-million-dollar business.

She isn't surrounded by legions of marketers and publicists.

In fact, Katie is shocked that people see her as a role model.

All she had was a never-quit attitude—and a blog.

When Dr. Oz, the popular health and fitness talk show host, asked his viewers to submit weight-loss stories, Katie offered her experience. To her, it was just another way to celebrate her achievement of transforming herself from the inside out. She pointed the Dr. Oz producers to her blog for day-by-day details.

A week later, a producer called to tell Katie she had been picked to come on the show. Katie listened as the producer told her that she had spent hours reading her blog. The producer said that every story, struggle, and victory added personality and dimension to a person she had never met. When she finished reading, she felt that Katie was her personal friend. Her submission was a no-brainer. They *had* to have Katie on the show.

After the Dr. Oz show aired, Katie's blog hit prime time. Corporate sponsors showed up to bankroll her 5K and half-marathon racing fees. A film team called with a request to document her life and training. Publishers are circling, looking for the opportunity to publish Katie's story.

During our interview, we probed, looking for a rare talent. While Katie had always kept a diary and enjoyed writing, she never viewed herself as a published author. She didn't have any special technical knowledge. She admitted that search queries on Google helped her through the basic setup on Blogger. Her blog is a simple journal with no fancy animations or jaw-dropping design. And she attracts 350,000 visitors a month!

Katie and other "everyday" people were the inspiration for *Born to Blog*.

Over the last three years, we've examined more than 500 blogs. We have personally consulted with more than 150 successful bloggers and dozens of corporations that depend on their blogs to build market share and sales. Our goal was to identify the core skills shared by successful bloggers.

At first, we expected that the skills would be special, unique talents unavailable to the average nonblogger. But we found something entirely different. The Internet is filled with bloggers just like Katie. We learned that blogging isn't an elite marketing strategy reserved for highly trained authors, journalists, and creative savants. It's a natural form of communication with skills preprogrammed into us all. You practice these skills every day. You just need to know how to summon them and put them to work.

We'll explore each skill in detail, but here's the nickel tour.

SKILL 1: DREAMING

You can't help but dream. During the day, you automatically start imagining a new future or relive and learn from past events. Dreaming is so reflexive that we create intricate systems to prevent us from daydreaming. Most of our slumber is filled with intricate worlds designed to reset our subconscious and organize our conscious thoughts.

We found that all bloggers have the ability to describe the world in their minds. They are willing to usher the public into their internal dramas and show others the insights they've uncovered. If you can dream, you can blog.

SKILL 2: STORYTELLING

Most of us believe that storytelling is reserved for Hollywood directors and Pixar animators. Not so. By noon, you've probably told several fairly complicated and entertaining stories. One story detailed your evening with the kids, a night at the club, or a Sunday afternoon watching the football game. Human beings are hardwired to pay attention to stories because this type of communication is suited to our love of metaphor, hidden meaning, and visual imagery. All bloggers tap into their natural ability to spin a great tale. They meld and hammer these stories into 600-word posts that can spark a revolution or soothe a grieving mother.

Can you tell a story? Yes. And you can blog.

SKILL 3: PERSUADING

It's nearly impossible for most people to leave a challenge to their reasoning unanswered. We feel that the other person deserves to hear our point of view. Not standing up for yourself is viewed as cowardly at best and hypocritical at worst. You probably have a variety of persuasive arguments oiled and primed for use. Business professionals have discussion points ready for difficult clients, difficult colleagues, difficult family members, and yes, difficult blog readers.

On the other hand, we are equally vigilant at being persuasive. We take pride in being able to nudge a fence-sitter to our side of an argument. While most are fairly well-practiced at avoiding contentious arguments, we can't resist taking a run at people who are unsure of their beliefs.

Some bloggers rely heavily on their persuasion skills. They write witty, satirical, and wickedly comedic blog posts that rip to the heart of their favorite subject. Sports, politics, marketing, religion, biking, and even nutrition harbor their fair share of persuaders and arguers who won't rest until you've heard their perspective.

Do you have passions and opinions? Then you can blog.

SKILL 4: TEACHING

Here is the beginning of a "can't miss" blog post: "How to . . ."

People turn to the web every day to learn and find answers to their questions. That's really what teaching is all about—using your experience to help people solve their problems.

There is nothing more rewarding than getting feedback that you actually helped somebody! Blogging is a great way to scale your natural inclination to help others by sharing your wisdom in a public forum. At least a third of our blog posts are generated by a reader question or comment. Simply being aware of those questions and using them as an opportunity to teach creates a wonderful opportunity to blog.

Online, the web is packed with blogs that share the latest largemouth bass fishing techniques, yoga positions, and money management tips. What questions do *your* readers have? If you can answer them, you can blog.

SKILL 5: CURATION

Assembling and organizing information is a skill that is hardwired. Your brain makes sense of the world by labeling and categorizing everything. Sometimes you have a specific interest in curating a certain object and your interest turns into a hobby. Many bloggers have learned how to turn their natural need to curate their world into popular and influential blogs.

Are there subjects that you can't resist critiquing, labeling, and categorizing into a list of the very best? Yes? My friend, you are blogger waiting to wow the world.

Bloggers tend to favor one set of skills over others. Some love to dream and tell stories. Others are gifted teachers and persuaders. You will have a preference as well. This book will help you develop all of your innate blogging skills and use them to attract an audience and achieve your goals . . . and perhaps transform your life.

Many times a blog's transformative power goes unnoticed.

During the interview with Katie, she frequently exhibited her need for privacy. Every word she said was examined and carefully vetted to ensure that she didn't reveal too much. You couldn't help but notice the dichotomy between Katie the mom and Katie the blogger.

Katie the blogger was fiercely transparent. Pictures of her broken jaw and post-tummy-tuck surgery were published for public consumption—albeit with a stern admonition not to post the photos on Pinterest.

Katie the mom seemed to shrink from the celebrity created by her appearance on *The Dr. Oz Show*.

How could a woman who spent a lifetime trying to blend into the background find the courage to live her life in front of 365,000 people every month?

"I guess it's my blog" Katie explains. "I feel that I owe it to my readers."

Katie isn't alone in this feeling. Millions are discovering that blogging isn't just a writing exercise—it's a life-changing opportunity.

The right technology has arrived at the right time to propel us forward. As Mark describes in his book *Return On Influence*, widespread access to high-speed Internet and free, easy-to-use publishing tools like blogging have created a new era of Citizen Influencers. It doesn't matter what you look like, where you were born, or if you have a college degree. Anybody can gain personal power on the web. Anybody can have a voice.

Influence has been democratized. We are all born to blog.

CHAPTER 4

Storytelling

A wedding proposal from Shahryar, King of Persia, was a death sentence.

Every morning, the king would marry a new virgin bride. For that day, he would devote every waking moment to the woman, showering her and her family with treasures from the king's vast storehouse of wealth. Every night the king would consummate the marriage. For most women, this would mark the beginning of a life of luxury. But every night the young queen would stay awake marking each hour, knowing that at sunrise she would be beheaded.

Within a few hours of his ex-wife's death, the king would marry another woman and begin the cruel ritual anew.

Infidelity had started the cycle of death.[1]

Shahryar's first bride had cheated on him. He never forgave her or forgot the blow to his pride. For 1,000 days, he wed and beheaded 1,000 virgins, reminding the nation of his humiliation and his determination never to be scorned again.

One morning, Scheherazade bowed at the king's feet and requested that she be allowed to spend one evening with him. Eyes wide in surprise, the stunned king granted her wish, mesmerized by her boldness. Didn't she know that sleeping with the king was a death sentence?

As dusk approached, Scheherazade followed the king into his bedchamber, reclined next to him, and began telling a story. Throughout the night, she wove a tale of adventure and intrigue. The king listened, captivated by the heroes and entranced by the villains.

An hour before sunrise, Scheherazade paused at a crucial moment in the story. She bowed her forehead to the floor and asked the king for forgiveness. Dawn was approaching, and she was too tired to continue. She promised to complete the story the following night if he would be merciful and grant her time to rest.

Still caught in the spell of her story, King Shahryar granted her wish. The next evening, Scheherazade finished her story. As the king marveled at the tale, Scheherazade began another—ending the story like the night before. Again she begged for time to rest—and repeated the process the following night.

Scheherazade continued her stories for 1,000 nights. On the 1,001st night, she finished her last story. No matter, the king had fallen in love with her, knowing that such a captivating and wise women would never break his heart. He spared her life, halting the ritual of death and making Scheherazade his queen.

Legend says that "The Seven Voyages of Sinbad the Sailor" and "Aladdin's Wonderful Lamp" were penned by Scheherazade and told to the king during those 1,000 nights.

Stories serve as skeleton keys that unlock our minds. We all can tell stories. We do every day. Unlike Scheherazade, our lives may not depend on our stories, but they still play an essential role in our lives.

STANFORD: My blog's goal is to make complicated marketing theories and strategies easy to understand within a few minutes. I've tried checklists, fancy illustrations, and video to simplify my subject. It took a year for me to see the power of stories. One day I was wrestling with how to convince my readers to take "outrageous action." I felt that many of them were playing it safe with their blogging, and I wanted to shake them a bit. When I arrived home that night, two of my three boys were playing outside.

As I climbed out of the car, I noticed that all of them were sporting freshly shaved Mohawk haircuts. The mix of emotions I felt ranged from surprise to irritation. In the moment, I wasn't willing to accept their "outrageous action." Immediately I realized that telling my readers this story would show them that I understood their own struggle with conformity. Even better, the Mohawk story would provide the right context for recommending how to blog with abandon.

We can't help but pay attention to stories because they are our primary way of understanding the world around us.

MARK: When I was writing *Return on Influence*, I was having trouble explaining the concept of reciprocity, a deeply ingrained human compulsion to return a favor.

On a trip to a rural village in North Carolina, I stumbled upon a store that had samples of all its mustards, jellies, and sauces out for unlimited tasting. After munching my way through the store, I felt I simply had to buy something from the store owner—I had to repay the gift of the delicious food—and walked out with $50 worth of groceries! A fun visit to a food store turned into a perfect example to demonstrate the concept that I had been struggling to explain. I was aware of my own experience and its power to tell a deeper story about human nature.

Some say that technological progress has outpaced our human evolution. Radio, TV, cinema, and YouTube all have given individuals progressively more prominent stages to tell their stories. Blogging is the latest technology in this journey. It also may be the most powerful.

The first blogs were online diaries. Their writers used them to chronicle their experiences and impressions about the world. One of the first bloggers described his fascination with software programming and the projects he was working on. At first, these blogs were cobbled together with HTML code. The launch of Blogger software made it easy for non-tech people to quickly pen their diary entries. Like the village campfire, these blogs were stories about the moral, emotional, and intellectual lessons learned during that day. Readers would browse the blogs gaining perspective from a worldwide community of diarists.

The ability to tell stories through blogs has also revolutionized marketing in some ways. People won't spend a second with an advertisement, but they'll spend 30 minutes with a great story. For many individuals and businesses, the blog is a way to tell that story and open the door in unexpected and human ways.

A company that has always done a great job of storytelling on its blog is General Electric. It's a multibillion-dollar, multinational company, but it has always done a masterful job of creating an emotional connection to its products, services, and history through stories.

In 2010, the company invited its scientist customers from around the world to submit the most beautiful medical photos they had taken with GE scanning electron microscopes. You know—those awesome close-up pictures you love in *National Geographic*. Then, they invited the customers with the winning entries to New York City but didn't tell them why.

They gathered the scientists as darkness fell upon Times Square and told them to "look up." GE had created a music video of the scientists' photos, and it was now playing on a gigantic screen above their heads. The GE team had the cameras rolling to capture the tears running down the faces of its astounded customers!

In this example, it was not an ad or a slick marketing brochure that told us that GE brings good things to life. It was a story, expressed through photography, art, music, and amazing storytelling all rolled into one company blog post.

Our conversations and research shows that you don't have to be a "great" storyteller. You don't have to be an accomplished playwright or understand the nuances of a riveting screenplay. The only prerequisite for blogging is the willingness to share your thoughts and opinions.

Think about your day. How do you feel? What caught your attention? What surprising tidbit did you learn about a colleague? How could you weave this into a story? If you are stuck, then shift your perspective. How would you describe your day to a significant other or best friend? Much easier, right? You probably automatically insert a moral or lesson to your day as well.

MARK: Many bloggers ask me how I can just stick to one topic on my blog—marketing—without being bored. But I'm never bored! I tell the story of marketing through my own varied interests and life experiences. For example, I loved how an art museum in Scotland was using digital technology to connect to kids, and so I did a video blog about it. I love working in the yard, and when a bunch of my new plants died, I was able to tell the story of a shocking customer service experience I had with the retailer that resonated with a lot of people. I've related how my love of sports translates to brand loyalty. On a trip to Russia, I was able to report on differences in advertising techniques I observed. So you see, I told my stories about art, gardening, sports, and travel to teach lessons about marketing. I'm always thinking in terms of stories!

Look again—your story along with its "moral" is a great blog post. The fascinating part is that you conduct this same storytelling process every day. The best bloggers learn to pay attention to daily epiphanies and quickly immortalize them in blog posts.

Among the billion people who have access to the Internet, there are more than a few people who will find your insights fascinating—perhaps even profound. They will value your experiences and want to hear more. They can't help themselves because your story will enrich their own.

Along with our urge to create heroes and villains comes the impulse to change our world.

TAKE ACTION

Begin to build a discipline of being aware of the stories in your life. Start to pay attention to how many stories you tell throughout your day to inform, entertain, explain, and teach. Simply make a note each time you tell a story. If it is something that is interesting to your real-world audience, it might entertain your online audience too. Is there a way to relate your story to a current event?

If there is a topic you would like to write about on your blog, think about personalizing it by connecting it to a story. Does your topic connect to:

- Another experience you had in your career?
- Lessons from a favorite hobby or sport?
- A story from your childhood?
- A favorite saying, story, or quote?
- A related example you have heard of from the news?[2]

Notes

[1] http://en.wikipedia.org/wiki/List_of_One_Thousand_and_One_Nights_characters#Shahry.C4.81r.

[2] http://en.wikipedia.org/wiki/Scheherazade.

CHAPTER 5

Dreaming

W e are hardwired to dream. Every moment is a desperate fight to keep our attention in the present. A half second of distraction shifts our mind to neutral and kicks on the "daydream." For a few moments—even a few minutes—we are lost in our own world. You've probably seen high-powered executives tune out in the middle of meetings, snatching a moment to romp in the playground of their own thoughts.

Although we chastise ourselves for dreaming too much, it's essential for business success. Everything of value in our world started at some point with an idle daydream. Dreaming helps us connect the dots. Dreaming is mandatory for seeing the world as it should be rather than how it is.

Thankfully, our ability to dream is planted deep within us. On a physiological level, dreaming is required for sanity. A person who cannot dream will die.

Bloggers who cannot dream wither away.

> **STANFORD:** I hit a dry patch about six months after starting *Pushing Social.* The blog was doing well and had started getting mentioned by other prominent bloggers. It seemed that everything was moving in the right direction.
>
> But the truth was that I hated writing. Every post seemed to be another dry rendition of the one before it. My readers were

annoying me. The entire social media scene seemed baseless and intellectually bankrupt.

I seriously debated giving up the blog and moving on. *Pushing Social* had started as an experiment, and I felt that I had nothing new to learn.

I went through this patch around the time of my family's annual camping trip. This trip is sacred for one reason: I get to fish as much as I want. And I do. I'm known as the unshaven fishing monk that spends hours reading the currents, water temperature, and lily pads in search of the epic largemouth bass.

During those long hours of drowning hundreds of night crawlers, I daydream. I ask myself important questions and search for the answers between long casts into the middle of a calm lake.

That year, I asked myself, "Why do I blog? What do I want to accomplish?"

Ironically, the so-called blogging guru had forgotten to ask himself these critical questions.

It took two days, but the answers floated to my conscious mind. I discovered that I wanted to live in a world where people could be paid handsomely to indulge their passions. I imagined people dreaming big and using their blogs to assemble teams of fellow visionaries.

I also saw how writing had deeply therapeutic benefits. My time touring the blogosphere had introduced me to cancer survivors, recovering alcoholics, bullied teens, and other people struggling to put their world back together again. Blogging helped these people make extraordinary changes in their lives.

I especially loved helping start-ups use blogs to avoid the expensive ad game and tell their company's story. As I sat on my bucket, watching a worm wiggle from the container and try to inch its way to freedom, I felt a new fire swell in my chest. My dreams were rekindling a deep urge to matter to real people conquering real challenges.

I grabbed my notebook and pen from the tackle box and scribbled a few blog post ideas. About an hour later, I looked up. I had sketched an entire year of blog posts, about 104 ideas that captured my passion for teaching ordinary people how to do extraordinary things.

I reeled in my line, surprised to see a bluegill dangling from the line, angry that he had been snagged for an hour.

I went on to have an amazing year. My readers noticed the rekindled voice in my posts. My readership tripled in just a few months.

Now, I spend every year by the lake dreaming about the future. You have the same opportunity. Everyone was born to dream.

Our society's habit of labeling people irks me. We are quick to label people as visionaries or dreamers. Unfortunately, you get the label of *visionary* if you make money and *dreamer* if your plans don't quite pan out! We can't seem to get it through our heads that labels only limit us.

I can see the doubt in my clients' eyes when I tell them that they should dream about the purpose of their blog. It's difficult for them to imagine the impact that dreaming has on their blog's voice, story, and impact.

I nudge them along with the question I asked by the fishing hole: Why do you blog?

Since we are social animals, we inevitably drift back to the core reason for publicly publishing our thoughts: feedback and validation.

We want to see how our dreams play out. We are drawn to the challenge of getting people's unvarnished opinions. Even more, we want to see if there is anyone else who shares our dreams.

Dreaming is an emotional exercise. Starting your blog by envisioning your goal infuses your writing with emotional impact. Readers can feel your intensity and respond. This give-and-take interaction is intimate, affirming, and powerful.

Sometimes letting your mind wander can produce the most interesting results.

> **MARK:** I had an idea for a blog post but didn't quite know how to express it. It had something to do with how very limited we are when we are expressing ourselves in little boxes on Facebook or in 140 characters in Twitter. We seem to take it for granted, but it really stymies creativity!
>
> I pretty much dropped the idea but caught myself daydreaming in a meeting. I started fantasizing about what people from our past would think about this new technology. Would they love it or hate it? What if you plopped an artist or writer from history down in front of Facebook? Then it hit me—that is exactly what I should do. I turned my daydream into reality by "interviewing" a dead artist, Andy Warhol, on his thoughts on Facebook. Turning a daydream into a reality resulted in a popular and creative post!

Business people often sniff at the "emotional stuff." They may approach a blog as just another marketing tool. Tell customers what you have to offer, and leave it to the economic laws of supply and demand. The argument is cold: "If I offer the right goods at the right price, I make a sale. People are rational actors."

However, other successful business owners see it differently.

Buy a pair of shoes from TOMS, and the company will give a new pair of shoes to a child in the developing world. As of April 2010, over 600,000 pairs of shoes have been given to needy children across the globe.

The shoe donations have been part of TOMS' story from the beginning. TOMS' founder, Blake Mycoskie, believes that many of the world's problems can be solved if corporations intentionally design charitable giving into their business models. TOMS' success shows that charity is good for the world and good for business.

TOMS' blog *One for One* shows readers how their purchases are changing the lives of children around the world. Every post gives you a glimpse into the day-to-day dreams of children across the world. The blog inducts its readers into the One for One movement and adds emotional power behind every customer purchase.

Kathy Cano-Murillo dreams about glitter . . . lots of it.

The founder of CraftyChica.com started blogging to feed her passion for art.

"I daydreamed about teaching classes on every continent and inspiring women everywhere to embrace the healing power of glitter," she said.

Yes, the healing power of glitter.

Kathy turned her dream into a bustling blog with more than 10,000 readers a month. Her blogs have also attracted national attention, leading to TV appearances and a book deal. She also sells her own Crafty Chica line to women nationwide.

Dreams were the starting points for these blogs and businesses. They can serve the same powerful role for you.

The dreams are locked inside of you waiting for permission to ignite your blog.

Sitting down and writing a blog post about those daydreams is great first step. It seems that once unleashed, people inevitably create blogs that propel them toward their goal.

The best part is that you don't need any special equipment, tools, or venture capital money to dream. You were born with all you need.

TAKE ACTION

Sometimes it takes a little quiet time to allow your dreams to come to the forefront. For Stanford, it is time at his favorite fishing hole. For Mark, it is hiking to a mountain stream. In our always-on, information-dense world, you may have to disconnect to get the breakthrough idea.

How do you get inspired? Do you schedule time to reflect and get reenergized? Are you in tune with your dreams, and do you give them the space they need to grow and turn into something great?

CHAPTER 6

Persuading

The achievements of Students for a Free Tibet
show that nonviolent action does work.

—The Dalai Lama

A search for "the most persuasive blogs" on Google returns an eclectic collection of blogging misfits and titans. Our search bounced from *PerezHilton*, dubbed the most hated blog in Hollywood, to *Boing Boing*, a smart, titillating mix of news and photos.

But are these blogs "persuasive?" It depends on your point of view. *Engadget*, a popular tech blog, could influence someone's decision to buy an iPhone over an Android, but does that decision really matter?

Quickly we saw that we needed to dig deeper and find people blogging about extraordinary things that impact people on a fundamental level.

The search took us to Tibet, specifically to a group called Students for a Free Tibet—a highly organized student-led movement focused on keeping the Tibetan people's struggle for independence alive.

The blog is the intellectual and logistical anchor for the student group. It persuades by educating visitors on the history of Tibet and pointing the light of world scrutiny on human rights violations in Tibet. Chapters from across the world can report on campaign efforts in their countries and cities.

In just 20 minutes, a reader understands why independence is long overdue for the Tibetan people and how to get involved in the cause.

This blog is making a difference by persuading through education.

Over the last five years, social organizations have adopted blogging as a rapid-response tool with an uncanny knack of establishing reader trust and rapport. The conversational, almost impromptu, nature of blogging cultivates an appreciation for simplicity over complexity.

Good thing. We tend to take action when we are given a clear reason.

Think about the last time you persuaded your friends to do something. I'm sure you used a simple formula: This is what I want to do. This is why you'll like it. This is what it will cost. What do you think? Nothing complicated about this approach.

Businesses are catching on. With the almost ubiquitous use of social media tools like Facebook and Twitter, business marketers can watch their customers interact with each other in real time. They can see how golf buddies trade putting tips and single moms share ways to balance work and home. From these observations, they've realized that friends and family are effective persuaders because they don't try. They just share their experiences. They are credible due to the investment they've made in their relationships.

Marketing strategists have found that persuasion works best when it doesn't look like a television ad. When surveyed, only 14 percent of respondents said they trust advertisements.[1]

That's probably why only 18 percent of TV campaigns generate a positive ROI.[2] Ouch. On the other hand, 90 percent of people agreed that they trust peer recommendations. It's not a big surprise that customers buy from people and companies they trust. Frequent, valuable interactions accelerate the trust-building process. This process has been dubbed *content marketing*, a strategy that builds customer trust with focused and relevant information. The technique relies proactively on the businesses' willingness to consistently publish information and engage in two-way dialogue over weeks, months, and years.

While 140-character tweets and Facebook updates play an important role, marketers rely on blogs to tell their story. We'll talk about specific blogging approaches in later chapters, but for now we'll recognize that blogs are the perfect tool for persuading customers, donors, and readers to consider a specific perspective. However, jamming sales messages into blog posts isn't persuasion. It's dumb. Building trust and sharing your thoughts just like you would with a friend works so much better.

During the lead-up to the 2007 presidential primaries, Hillary Clinton had secured the title of "presumptive" Democratic nominee. The formidable Clinton political machine had the money, connections, and organization to breeze through the fall, sweeping aside the relatively weak slate of Democratic contenders. Illinois Senator Barack Obama understood that fighting on Clinton's terms was a guaranteed way to lose. Drawing on lessons learned from his years as a community organizer, Obama looked for ways to make his case to voters. His campaign recruited Chris Hughes, a Facebook cofounder, to organize his online campaign efforts.[3] One of the online team's first programs was to set up a blog.

Obama's blog showcased stories from grassroots rallies in battleground states. Obama frequently recorded and posted quick videos explaining his position on issues and encouraging his swelling number of volunteers. Chris Hughes's team worked hard to simplify the message and deliver the right information to the right voter at the right time.

Soon word spread about Obama's sophisticated online strategy, and other candidates, including Clinton, quickly set up their own blog and outreach efforts. None of the other candidates understood the strategy, however. They didn't invest time in setting up genuine relationships. Unlike Obama, who was able to raise more than $500 million from donors, $25 at a time, Clinton managed to raise a fraction of that amount.

By February 2008, Obama's blog, social media outreach, and savvy online ad spending pushed him past Clinton. Clinton endorsed Obama at the Democratic National Convention and went on to join President Obama's cabinet as secretary of state.

Obama understood that persuasion is easy once you have a relationship. His team members used their natural ability to share why they believed in Obama's candidacy. Their genuine respect for and belief in Obama translated into a firm foundation of trust when the campaign began asking for donations.

The Obama campaign and other candidates that have since emulated his approach drew on the same skills that you use every day: finding common ground, building a relationship, and simply making your case for what you like, value, and believe in.

MARK: The problem with creating persuasive blog posts is that you rarely know when you are having an impact—whether you are actually being persuasive at all. We may not have the benefit of feedback from a national presidential campaign!

A rule of thumb is that only about 2 percent of your readers leave comments. That's a generalization that I have found holds up across many types of blogs. Readers may be too busy, too shy, or just not interested enough to comment.

In addition to only hearing from a small minority of your readers, there is a big difference between a "comment" on the topic and real feedback on how you are doing as blogger—if you are making a dent in the way people really act and think.

Early on in my blogging career, I realized that if I was going to make truly meaningful connections with these strangers popping in on my blog, I was going to have to make an effort to get to know them better. So I started to call them. And what an amazing experience that was!

I made a goal to call at least three of my blog readers per week over a period of a couple of months, and by far the overwhelming lesson I learned was, yes, I was having an impact in many unexpected ways.

I'll never forget a call I had with Caroline Di Diego, a businessperson and entrepreneur who left many interesting comments on my blog. She told me in great detail how one quite obscure blog post had really changed her outlook on business and marketing. Although the post had run two years before, she could still recall its lessons and it still affects her even to this day.

This meant so much to me because I had been particularly proud of that blog post, but it had not been a popular post in terms of how much it had been shared. In fact, I was so disappointed by the reaction to this thoughtful post that I wondered why I was blogging at all.

Caroline's reaction gave me a new energy, a new commitment to blogging, because she made me realize that even though I might not hear it every day, I am having an impact.

STANFORD: When I created *Pushing Social*, I wanted to persuade business thinkers to take a realistic approach to social media. I felt that social media was being overrun by people who valued "comfort words" over specific business strategies and tactics. At first, I didn't believe that I could persuade anyone. I thought you had to be a sophisticated wordsmith who could subtly manipulate readers. I thought persuasion was a specific talent that either you had or you didn't have. I didn't even try to persuade my readers. I just started writing.

A few months after starting the blog, I began getting comments from people thanking me for changing their position on a subject. Shocked, I read through my blog posts and saw that I was working hard to persuade my readers. Although I wasn't specifically trying to convince them, I was still advocating my position, providing evidence, and encouraging my readers to challenge my viewpoints. Over time, as relationships and trust grew, my readers began identifying themselves with my no-nonsense approach to social business and marketing.

I realized that I couldn't "turn off" my urge to persuade. It was natural. The stronger I felt about a subject, the more I pushed my viewpoint. Once I realized this, I started to see the same pattern in other blogs. Everyone from fitness trainers to wine connoisseurs uses their blogs to explain their point of view and gather support.

TAKE ACTION

Taking a stand in a very public forum can be nerve-racking. But it can also be a lot of fun and one of the most rewarding experiences a blogger can have.

There is no way to experience this other than to just try it. Take a stand on an issue and take a shot at a persuasive blog post. If you want feedback on it, try calling a few of your readers to see what they thought. You might be surprised at how persuasive you really are!

Dreaming, storytelling, and persuasion aren't the only skills used by bloggers. They also rely on another preprogrammed blogging skill that transforms them from writers into leaders.

Notes

[1] See http://blog.nielsen.com/nielsenwire/consumer/global -advertising-consumers-trust-real-friends-and-virtual -strangers-the-most.

[2] Larry Weber, *Marketing to the Social Web*, Wiley Publishing, 2007.

[3] See http://fastcompany.com/1207594/how-chris-hughes-helped -launch-facebook-and-barack-obama-campaign.

CHAPTER 7

Teaching

Parents teach their children. Leaders build world-class organizations by mentoring key team members. Bloggers share their lessons with their readers. We are teaching even we don't think about it.

Our research and observations show three types of day-to-day teaching encounters: teaching by doing, conversation, and coaching or mentoring.

TEACHING BY DOING

You are being watched. Your colleagues observe your behavior in meetings. Your neighbors watch you play with your children. Your spouse watches your reaction to financial pressure. Although you aren't teaching through instruction, you are teaching by example.

Living is the primary way bloggers teach their audiences. Cancer survivors, obese mothers, adrenaline seekers, and others share their lives and their reaction to life's curveballs. Their actions become examples, and those examples become lessons for us to learn from.

> **STAN:** I spent a lot of time tinkering and experimenting with blogging when I first started *Pushing Social*. The blog's layout would change almost daily. I would try different post headlines, often within a few hours of publishing them. Readers tell me that they

learned the most from watching me make these changes. They were able to see the method to my madness and put what they learned to use.

CONVERSATION

Listen to the world around you. While waiting in line, listen to the conversations between parents, kids, and couples. It's surprising how much information we share about one another. Listen a little closer, and you'll also hear people constantly teaching through casual conversation.

> **STAN:** During one meeting, I learned how to take screenshots on my iPhone, the best way to cook beef jerky, how to use Evernote to gather research, and the best website for finding robot kits for my boys. Sure, I won't use most of these lessons, but the conversation revealed four people who were fantastic conversational teachers.

You can see conversational learning by paying attention to blog comments. It's fascinating to see how the writer relaxes and opens up with readers when responding to comments. The writer often teaches more through these unguarded moments than he or she did in the post. Readers use the comments to expand on the post, teaching fellow readers valuable information. Few of these people would call themselves teachers, but teaching is exactly what they are doing.

> **MARK:** My blog has a worldwide audience, so in the original post I make an effort to be very simple, free of regional colloquialisms, and very careful with humor that may not translate well to other cultures. But responding to comments is more like

chatting with friends. For me, that's where a lot of the teaching takes place.

COACHING OR MENTORING

Fewer people are in coaching or mentoring situations. Coaching requires the student and coach to adopt formal roles where one is committed to sharing knowledge with the other. The coach has to demonstrate comprehensive experience and have a track record of success.

However you can still see a form of coaching in interactions between managers and team members and parents and children. When they think of teaching, this is what people think of along with formal teaching roles. While most tend to shy away from this form of teaching, we often can easily slip into the role in the right situation.

Some of the best bloggers have a natural bias for teaching. They feel comfortable whipping out how-to posts and publishing checklists. As natural learners, we tend to flock to these blogs because they promise preorganized information that we can quickly process and evaluate.

It's important to realize that living and conversation are even more effective than formal mentoring. We tend to value "walking the walk" rather than "talking the talk." The best teachers can back up their rhetoric with an authentic life.

You may not be a formal teacher or coach, but it's likely that you are a formidable role model.

Tim Ferriss, the author of *The 4-Hour Workweek*, is an amazing mentor and teacher, and his subsequent book, *The 4-Hour Body*, demonstrates his willingness to walk the walk.

Over the years, Ferriss has undergone a battery of exhaustive and painful experiments to refine and build his body.

He's documented each of these tests and put the results in his book. Over the same time, he's shared his experiences on his blog.

A glance at the comments on the blog shows that his readers appreciate his willingness to be a human guinea pig for them. I'm convinced that he has legions of fans and advocates because he is willing to live his life in public and let us learn from his example.

YOU ARE TEACHING NOW

Embracing your innate desire to teach is a quick way to get your blog noticed. Your readers want to learn. They are looking for the right teacher who is down-to-earth, knowledgeable, and passionate about the subject. Most likely you are already teaching friends and family. It's time to pour that energy into your blog.

If you have a natural inclination to teach, feed that desire by finding new ways to approach your subject.

If you're answering questions at work or with fellow hobbyists, you're teaching. Start answering those questions in writing, and you're blogging!

CHAPTER 8

Curation

Swedish designer Tina Roth Eisenberg dutifully updates her blog, *swissmiss* (www.swiss-miss.com), with examples of intelligent product design. Although there are millions of well-designed products, only a few meet Eisenberg's definition of *intelligent* and are showcased on her blog. Even though *swissmiss* is Eisenberg's personal "design journal," over 1 million people visit the blog every month to see what she's found. *swissmiss* and others like *Candy Snob* (candysnob.com), and *MLB Trade Rumors* (mlbtrade-rumors.com) are successful examples of the latest evolution in blogging—curation.

Spend 10 minutes reading about social media, and you'll trip over the term *curation*. Many believe that curation is just a fancy way to say "collecting." No, curation is much more important.

WHAT IS CURATION?

Curation is methodical—even obsessive—about building unique collections of content. The term comes from the art world, where gallery owners are revered for their ability to gather and present collections of art. Curating is critical to the artist's success. A disjointed collection taints the art and tarnishes the curator's reputation. Art lovers rely on curators to filter the world of choices and present the best examples of the best.

Taken into the online world, curating describes compiling a list of the best information about a subject. Think of articles, photos, and songs as art, the blog as the gallery, and the blogger as the gallery owner.

Pinterest launched in January 2010 with a simple mission—make it easy for people to express themselves, their dreams and desires, visually. Pinterest gambled on the notion that people love collecting photos that express their personality. The founders used a corkboard motif to brilliantly illustrate what they wanted users to do—pin photos into themed collections.

Pinterest demonstrates that curating is as natural for us as telling stories and teaching our children. Many of us love to passionately categorize, prune, and grow our hobbies.

The curation gene is alive and kicking among top bloggers. In almost every subject, you'll find bloggers publishing volumes of "list posts" that itemize carefully curated information. Sites like *12 Most* are built on the popularity of the list post and its ability to scratch our curation itch. Other popular sites like *Boing Boing* curate weird news items and photos. And of course, *LOLCats* shows that just about any interest can be curated by an observant blogger.

Somewhere on the web, people are curating their favorite news items on the most amazing, most disturbing, most entertaining, and most fun content they can find.

There are two important benefits to readers of curated blogs. First, they help connect people with similar passions. Second, they can save people a lot of time. For example, if you are looking for the latest information on a topic, why spend time searching when you can feed your need from a trusted expert who is already doing the heavy lifting for you?

There are also some unique benefits to the blogger. First, if you have difficulty writing, curating may be a legitimate way to get in the game. Second, a side benefit is that it will help you build your online network as people will naturally be attracted to your specific niche subject.

RECOGNIZING YOUR KNACK FOR CURATION

Of all the natural blogging skills, curation may be hardest to recognize. Many times curation works alongside teaching, with teaching taking the prominent role. For example, penny-pinching bloggers teach about saving money while curating lists of coupon sites and coupon-friendly stores. On the surface these bloggers are great teachers, but their obsession is curating comprehensive lists of money-saving tips and tools.

If you have a knack for teaching, take another look and see if you are also a curator in disguise.

Although curation is less dependent on creating original content, a skillfully curated blog may actually take more time than writing something yourself!

We've finished an examination of each of the skills. Have you identified your natural blogging skill yet? Just in case, we'll give you a quick tool to put you on the right track so you can unleash your inner blogger!

CHAPTER 9

Discovering Your Blogging Skills

You have a natural preference for one of the five skills and can quickly pinpoint that skill by thinking about the types of movies, books, and people you are drawn to. Storytellers tend to favor fiction, watch dramas, and hang out with friends who love a great story. Natural persuaders can't resist documentaries and nonfiction, and they populate their dinner parties with people who have strong opinions. Even though you may have a blend of two or three skills, you will lean on one just as you prefer your right or left hand.

STANFORD: When I first started blogging, I wrote provocative posts that relied on taking a contrarian position. A month of that left me disillusioned. I felt out of sync with my subject and thought that blogging wasn't the best way to express myself. That day by the lake helped me connect with my dreamer and teacher skill sets. Changing my focus unleashed a torrent of new ideas. Posts were easy to write because I used my natural voice and style.

MARK: I had a similar experience when I pushed myself out of my natural skill set of storyteller and teacher. When I was starting out, I noticed that many blogs featured product reviews where the writers tried to persuade readers why they should buy or not buy a certain gadget or service. I was still finding my way in the blogging business and decided that I needed to do this too.

What a disaster! First, I am not a very technical person. I really didn't have time to do a thorough evaluation of these products, and I found out I hated doing these reviews! But most important, this form of blogging was simply incongruent with my personal style. I tend to be a conversation starter. I don't see myself in a role of telling anybody what to do or not do. I simply love to provide new angles for people to think about and let them come to their own conclusions. The reviews didn't work, but we all learn by doing, right?

Now that we've identified dreaming, storytelling, persuading, teaching, and curation, let's see which skill you favor. Take the short Core Blogging Skill Preference Quiz that follows.

BORN TO BLOG SKILLS QUIZ

Score each question: 1 = Never, 2 = Rarely, 3 = Sometimes, 4 = Frequently, 5 = Very Frequently. Add the points in each section get your score for that skill.

DREAMER
1. Do you approach problems with a blank slate, preferring to try new approaches?   _____

2. Are you suspicious of rules of thumb, believing that they inhibit your creativity?   _____

3. Are you drawn to people and leaders who focus on innovation and creative thinking?   _____

4. Have you been labeled as an idealist and been encouraged to keep your feet on the ground?   _____

Score: _____

STORYTELLER
1. Do you reflexively identify the characters and plot in day-to-day situations?   _____

2. Are you the designated "talker" in group settings?   _____

3. Are you nurturing a dream of publishing a novel?   _____

4. Are fiction books at the top of your "best books" list?   _____

Score: _____

PERSUADER
1. Do you have to "hold your tongue" at dinner parties to avoid offending guests?   _____

2. Do your friends know exactly where you stand on political and religious issues?   _____

3. Are you comfortable with debate and conflict?   _____

4. Do you distrust people who are unwilling to stand up for what they believe?   _____

Score: _____

TEACHER

1. Do you like process, steps, and clear instructions? _____

2. Do you get a thrill out of showing someone a
new skill? _____

3. Do you have a knack for explaining complicated
subjects? _____

4. Are you often asked to lead discussions or present
new material? _____

Score: _____

CURATOR

1. Do you love to collect and organize unique objects,
stories, or experiences? _____

2. Do people mention your "good taste" and "eye for
detail"? _____

3. Do you feel comfortable with making subject-based
lists? _____

4. Do you feel drawn to art, fashion, photography, and
other creative pursuits? _____

Score: _____

Review your scores and pay special attention to the areas where you scored the highest. Areas where you scored 16 or higher indicate a strong preference for that skill. Scores of 8 or lower for an area point to a weak preference for the skill.

You may have several areas with relatively high scores. This means that you have a couple of core skills to draw upon. That's perfectly normal, and you will have more content writing options and appeal to a broader audience.

UNDERSTANDING YOUR SKILLS

The important point is to understand your strong skills and be aware of skills you may be weak in. For example, you may find it difficult to write a "how-to" blog post if you scored low for the teacher skill.

If you already have a blog, compare your skill preference to the type of posts on your blog. If you are struggle with writing blog posts, it's likely that you aren't using your dominant skill. Most often this happens when a person tries to copy another blogger's style. Is it time to make an adjustment?

New bloggers can get focused and use the skill test to start out strong with blog posts that match up with their particular skill preference. Steer clear of posts that require proficiency with a skill that you are weak in. You don't have to ignore these areas forever; just get momentum going with the stronger posts. Work on strengthening other areas as you get more comfortable with blogging and get a feel for your audience's needs.

Now let's get into some practical ideas on how to start, maintain, and leverage these powerful skills on a business blog.

CHAPTER 10

Why Your Business Should Blog

There is probably no social media platform that strikes fear in the heart of businesses more than a blog. Facebook is just . . . so friendly. And you can't do too much damage in 140 characters on Twitter, can you? The buttoned-up approach of LinkedIn is easy for most businesses to comprehend.

But blogs? Who has the time to blog? What would *we* have to write about?

Without question, blogs offer the most potential value to most businesses. Many consultants will have a business start there on a social media strategy. Not Facebook. Not Twitter. A blog. If content is the fuel that runs the social web, then blogs are the engine.

BUSINESS BENEFITS OF BLOGGING

Let's look at a few of the solid business benefits of blogging.

- **Brand awareness.** The last decade has ushered in an age of hypercompetition. It's getting harder to use traditional media to break through the noise and make an impact. A blog can help you get noticed by giving your company a way to tell its story. Creating a voice of authority in your industry can help you create a sustainable point of differentiation.

- **Direct sales.** A blog is valuable real estate. If you create highly sought-after content, you are going to be attracting high-potential prospects. Why not feature ads on your blog that direct leads to new products and services? Marriott sells millions of dollars of hotel bookings through its blog. Software giant SAP has several ads on every blog promoting upcoming training sessions.
- **Indirect sales.** Blogs are great "gateway" platforms for initiating relationships that later lead to sales. Blogs allow you to showcase what you're really made of better than a static website. Blog-only special offers, giveaways, and exclusive deals can be used to get prospect e-mail addresses that can be used for follow-up e-mail marketing.
- **Sales support.** Sales teams can use blog posts to beef up presentations and sales literature. Sales professionals often author their own blog posts based on questions they hear in the field. Why not use links to blog posts to answer common customer service questions? Blog posts become a library of helpful answers.
- **Research and development.** Companies like Fiskars, AT&T, Starbucks, and Caterpillar use their blogs as a way to unearth customer needs, ideas, and unmet desires that may turn into the next new product or service.
- **Public relations.** The news media are all over company blogs, seeking ideas for news stories, quotes, or sources. The rich content of blogs can become a

news story. It's probably not going to happen with a Facebook post or tweet!

- **Crisis management.** In the course of events of every company, eventually something goes wrong. Today, companies frequently use blogs to tell their side of the story or to keep the public apprised of developing news in a timely fashion.
- **Search engine traffic.** Perhaps the most powerful benefit of blogs accrues to a company even if nobody reads the blog—search engine benefits. Google loves blogs because they are updated regularly with new information relevant to its search customers. HubSpot research noted that company websites with blogs get 55 percent more traffic than websites without blogs.

You might be thinking that producing great content with these kinds of results is easy for big businesses with big budgets—and certainly we would not turn down a large budget if offered it! But small businesses can have an edge too. There is nothing more passionate or interesting than an insider view written by a company's founder. It may not be glitzy, but it can be exceptional content, and it doesn't break the bank, either.

Entrepreneur Stephen Cronk quit his executive job in London to follow his dream of starting a winery in Provence. He has a bootstrapper's budget but has captured the imagination of every entrepreneur who ever wanted to chuck a company job and follow his or her dream. Through a series of video blogs, Stephen does a masterful job of telling the ups and downs of his business adventures with Mirabeau Wine—the thrill of having the first bottles come off the filling line, the magic of standing atop a harvesting machine as the sun comes up over the Provençal hills, the exasperation of French government paperwork, the desperation when his expensive labels come back from the printer with an error.

The blog is a reality series of a business adventure unfolding before the reader that builds a strong emotional connection to the winery and its owner. And what does it cost Stephen? Nothing but a little time.

Similarly, Helen Brown, founder of The Helen Brown Group, is using her company blog to establish a voice of authority in the nonprofit sector. She blogs about donor research and fund-raising best practices. At first she struggled with the commitment it takes to blog, but she has now come to enjoy it as she found her "voice" and receives positive customer feedback. Although her company is small, she has skillfully used the channel to enhance her reputation in a manner that has led to speaking invitations, new customer contacts, and a book deal.

In the B2B sector, MLT Creative in Atlanta is a boutique marketing firm that has realized big results from its award-winning blog. Blogging is perfect in the B2B world, where the sales cycle is long and relationships matter. MLT involves nearly every employee in its blogging efforts and has expertly woven blog analytics into its sales funnel with inbound marketing software. By tracking certain blog-reading patterns, MLT can prequalify leads to decrease sales costs and improve the sales conversion rate.

THE BLOGGING THREE STOOGES

Despite these powerful benefits, it's often difficult for classically trained business (or nonprofit) people to get their head around blogging. For them, blogging might be situated somewhere between an advertorial and a press release. The corporate team understands that a blog should be conversational and informal but worries that being too "flip" with customers could undermine the company's brand reputation. Often the marketing team is tasked with coming up with a blog that is slightly less formal than the company's website. Or worse, the blog is shipped off wholesale to the advertising agency as a "campaign tool."

The result of this hodgepodge approach is rehashed press releases, thinly veiled sales pitches, and irrelevant "on the ground" reports about the company holiday party. Soon the folks looking after the bottom line begin to question the money invested in the blog and get minimal push-back from the overworked marketing team. The blog posting schedule drops from two mediocre posts a week to a single irrelevant post a month. Inevitably an enlightened manager figures that the company can handle "content marketing" 140 characters at a time on Twitter and the blog is scuttled.

We've watched this unfortunate blog death spiral many times. In every situation, there was a solid business case for publishing a blog. In fact, a well-executed blog could have contributed to bottom-line performance and market leadership. However, the mistake in every case was poor planning in three areas—the blogging three stooges!

Stooge 1: Wrong Purpose

Blogging expresses your business's personality. Social media is making personal interactions the new way to build brand loyalty. Your customers will arrive at your blog hoping to see "the other you," the easygoing person behind the brand. They aren't looking for a slightly better-looking website— they want a lot more. Effective blogs are the headquarters for a company's online conversation with its customers. A great business blog is like a campfire. Campfires are wonderful places to tell stories, share "getting to know you" information, and create deeper relationship bonds. If you set up a blog, you don't want to be the obnoxious one trying to dominate the conversation with sales pitches.

Another common problem is unrealistic expectations. Some businesses want to check a box so they can join the hallowed social media conversation everybody seems to be talking about. They are setting themselves up for disappointment. Blogging may take months of patience, commitment, and consistent execution before most companies begin to get traction from the effort.

If you can't or won't commit to sharing your company's story, people, culture, and approach with your customers, then do not start a blog. Your website and other marketing literature are already delivering the company line. It sounds radical, but blogging benefits only accrue to businesses that start with the right purpose and approach.

Stooge 2: Wrong Content

Content is simply the words, visuals, and media you use to communicate with your customer. On the social web, content is the catalyst that makes things happen. Great content is a radical evolutionary step-up from your company newsletters and e-mails. Great content has a different goal.

An e-mail or financial report might represent the monotone of typical corporate content. But great content turns that one-note script into a musical! Regular content shows a picture; great content turns the picture into a slideshow or video. A table of numbers is regular content; the same table transformed into an exciting infographic is great content.

Neil Patel, founder of Crazy Egg and Kissmetrics, writes one of the best blogs on online marketing. Each post is meticulously researched and beautifully written. When you read Neil's post, you know you are getting a complete explanation. Neil writes great content.

Another excellent example is Glenn Allsopp, ViperChill. com's publisher. Glenn is known for writing one "epic" post a month. His posts often average 9 or 10 pages. Every paragraph is packed with amazing insights and practical tips. Even though Glenn covers subjects similar to those on other websites, you are drawn to his exhaustively detailed and well-crafted posts. Glenn writes great content.

Johnson & Johnson's content creators don't just write something about how to talk to a child about surgery. They show you in the stories they tell through their amazing video content. This storytelling effectively communicates the values of the company in a way that grabs your heart and pulls you in.

You don't have to have a huge budget to create great content. In fact, we've discovered that most businesses have great content locked in various departments of their businesses just waiting to be featured in a blog. In a moment, we'll talk about how to find and unlock that content.

Stooge 3: Wrong People

Most companies assign blogging responsibilities to their PR department. The PR department then looks to an outside agency for writers. These writers often can write television scripts or magazine ads, but they fail miserably with blog writing. The blogs end up sounding too clinical and generic, gutting the blog of any personality.

In the book *Marketing in the Round*, authors Gini Dietrich and Geoff Livingston point out that many businesses still sequester their blogging and social media programs in one marketing silo. Other parts of the business are ignored or overlooked. This means that PR and corporate communications departments have little impact on the marketing department initiatives.

Many times, the best blog contributors are trapped in organizational silos and are never asked to author content for the blog.

Businesses that see their blog as a relationship-building platform will look for ways to break down the organization's silos and eventually make blogging a team sport.

We're not arguing that marketing shouldn't be the champion and center of excellence for blogging (quite the opposite). But, whether the responsibility for blogging is with PR, marketing, or customer service, the organization should work at encouraging enthusiastic people throughout the organization to contribute.

Are you fired up about blogging for your business? Of course you are. Let's go down another layer and start exploring some practical approaches to corporate blogging.

CHAPTER 11

Corporate Blogging's Most Common Questions

L et's tackle some of the common questions about business blogging. While a quick search on any of these questions would serve up thousands of opinions, we will offer the most practical and actionable options.

WHO "OWNS" THE BLOG?

This is a contentious and emotional debate at many companies, and it usually comes down to Public Relations versus Marketing.

Responsibility for your blog lies with the people responsible for communicating the business's story to its customers. Most blogs are used to try to create an action among the readers, who are potential customers, and that sounds like a marketing function.

It's less important who actually does the writing. Many employees and departments can be involved. In fact, the more the merrier. But at the end of the day Marketing should probably own the oversight and strategy at most companies.

HOW DO I MEASURE THE SUCCESS OF MY BLOG?

First, you will need to agree on the blog's objective. This objective should be an extension of your overall marketing strategy. An easy way to think about this is to ask, after people read our blog, what action would we like them to eventually take, or what goal would we like to accomplish?

For example, if your marketing objective is "to achieve a top position on your target customer's consideration list," then your blog's objective could be "increase the number of product information downloads by 50 percent," or "double the number of website customer inquiries."

After identifying the objective, select the metrics that accurately reflect performance. The good news is that there are so much data available on blog usage that this is one of the most measurable forms of marketing communication. For instance, with Google Analytics, Google's free web tracking service, you can track:

- Unique visitors: how many people visited your blog
- Page views: how often blog pages were visited for a specific time period
- Time on page: how long readers stayed on a specific page
- Bounce rate: how many left your blog without visiting another page

You can also get highly specific by seeing how many people visited a sales-oriented site after visiting the blog, or how many people clicked on an offer or discount you offered through your blog. If you are trying to establish thought leadership in your industry (a perfect role for the blog), the amount of time people are spending on your blog posts would be a good indicator that your message is getting through.

These are just a sample of the many useful metrics Google Analytics provides. You should pick the metric that most closely tracks the behavior you want to influence.

HOW DO I DEVELOP A CONTENT PLAN?

A content plan is a document that outlines blog topics, dictates publishing frequency, and helps coordinate writing and creative resources. This document is critical for a successful blogging program, especially if you have a long approval time for posts and if you have multiple bloggers trying to coordinate a schedule.

Your content plan should have the following elements:

- **Objectives:** Clearly outline your blog's objectives. These objectives guide content choices.
- **Audience:** Describe your ideal reader. Is it a CEO? A time-starved dad? A procurement manager? A career women looking for balance? The reader description will guide blog post subject selection and brainstorming.
- **Core topics:** List the core topics that matter to your reader. Focus on answering questions that your ideal reader will have about your product.
- **Quarterly blog post calendar:** Brainstorm blog posts and organize them into a three-month calendar. Start with publishing once a week. Add an additional post per week if you have the content and resources.
- **Roles and responsibilities:** Decide who will write each post and the process for approvals (managerial and legal).

Distribute the content plan and refine it to reflect any new changes in priorities. Use the plan to educate other company departments and possibly also to solicit post contributions.

One caution: Do not become overly wedded to the content plan. Have the flexibility to respond to external events and ideas to present relevant and timely content to your readers.

HOW OFTEN SHOULD WE BLOG?

Throughout this book, we emphasize the importance of consistency. Consistency contributes to search engine optimization (SEO) value, builds a loyal readership, and helps you improve as a communicator.

The amount of blogging appropriate for your business depends on your strategy. For example, a company that creates a lot of research and has to put a lot of effort into long and detailed posts might create just one major post per month. A small business featuring new craft ideas might blog once a week. A B2B company introducing many new high-tech solutions might create content a couple of times a week. A company that is curating content across an industry by summarizing major news events might provide this service every day. Some media companies post multiple times each day.

In general, as long as you are providing relevant, interesting, timely, and entertaining content, more is usually better as long as your customers don't complain that it's too much. Ask your audience how much content they would like to see. Begin polling about your blog in customer surveys to make sure you're staying on course.

DO I WRITE MYSELF OR OUTSOURCE?

Telling your businesses story should be core internal discipline. However, realistically this is difficult to pull off all the time. Many purists may scoff at the idea of hiring writers, but in some cases this can be a practical approach. Outsourcing your writing to a contractor that works closely with your team can be an effective solution, especially if writing is a chore for employees.

Your marketing agency can be a key partner for marshaling creative and editorial assets. These assets are valuable for creating a unique look and feel for your blog. The agency can also assist with creating a consistent look between your blog and other marketing platforms such as your website, print, and direct mail programs. Remember that you can repurpose content from your blog into many of these other marketing channels.

You will still need to be the "coach" for your blogging effort. While your agency can offer specialized resources, do not turn its assistance into a crutch. Remember that blogging works only when it's closely aligned with the vision, voice, and culture of your organization. You are the expert here, not your agency

WE'RE ALREADY BUSY—HOW DO WE FIND THE TIME TO BLOG?

This is a very common issue. It just doesn't seem fair to burden an already overloaded team with more work.

Our advice is that social media content creation should not be an "add-on." Maybe it's time for other activities to go away so you can redistribute your resources to work on the new media channels. For example, research shows that many segments of the population are spending less time with newspapers, television, and even websites. If this is where you are spending most of your marketing resources, maybe it's time to take a fresh look at your budget.

In a recent survey among U.K. procurement professionals, blogs were considered to be the most credible source of information early in the buying process—even above word-of-mouth recommendations. Why? Because bloggers are seen as trustworthy, passionate experts who stake their reputation on their writing every day.

Blogging offers too many business benefits to ignore.

WHAT HAPPENS IF WE GET NEGATIVE COMMENTS?

Perhaps there is nothing more frightening to a company than opening itself up to feedback and comments. Comments can be fun and inspiring when the news is positive and a legal nightmare if it turns sour. Here are a couple of best practice ideas about negative blog comments:

- Normally, negative comments should be regarded as a gift. If a person has a legitimate complaint, at least he or she is bringing it to your turf instead of spreading negative information around the marketplace.
- 98 percent of the time, the person just wants to be acknowledged. If you simply say, "We hear you, we're taking action, we're sorry," that usually handles the problem.
- Like any business, there is a small percentage of people who hate you just because they want to hate you, and nothing you say is going to matter. If you have an established blog with a loyal community, chances are your readers will come to your defense if the hate

comments persist, and that usually shuts it down. If it gets too bad, simply delete the comments. A company is not a democracy, and neither is a blog.

- Negative comments are not necessarily a bad thing. It adds credibility to your communication effort. A hotel chain recently told us that it actually likes a few negative reviews on its site because it shows that it's not edited, and this provides more weight to the many positive comments.
- In all cases, follow legal guidelines around content and blog comments. For example, the Mayo Clinic has many blogs on various health subjects, but its writers rarely answer comments due to regulations and guidelines about dispensing medical advice.
- Every company should have a social media policy with clear directions on the chain of command and crisis strategy if something blows up. This should be in place whether you decide to blog or not because detractors can show up any place on the web today.

Usually the fear of negative comments is unfounded, and you'll probably see this for yourself as you gain experience in the space.

CHAPTER 12

The Minimum Viable Blog

It's easy to overcomplicate blogging. It's not unusual for business teams to spend months finessing every detail. They create elaborate editorial calendars, commission infographics, and develop byzantine policies and legal procedures for publishing. Many of these blogs buckle under their own load.

That's a shame because blogging is simple—at least the formula for building and growing a blog is simple.

The most effective blogs are managed using minimal guidelines and straightforward objectives. They evolve rapidly and quickly gather a community of contributors. Blog posts are consistent and compelling. The blogging team is motivated and often breaks down organizational barriers to find the best content possible.

These blogs instinctively follow many of the core principles articulated in Eric Ries's landmark book *The Lean Startup*. In the book, Eric encourages start-ups to create a minimum viable product (MVP). The MVP is a stripped-down product designed to test market response. It's created with minimum functionality and even less budget. The MVP allows the start-up to see if it is solving a real marketplace problem before millions of dollars in capital and manpower is invested.

"LEAN THINKING"

Inspired by this approach, we've designed the MVB, or the minimum viable blog. Like its cousin the MVP, the minimum viable blog follows a "lean thinking" playbook.

Rapid Development

The MVB is designed using open source software such as WordPress to quickly build the core functionality of the blog. The MVB is simply a platform for the blog post and comments section with bare-bones navigation and sidebar functionality. The MVB can be created for less than $200 and can usually be integrated into existing websites for a little more investment from the IT department or your friendly neighborhood web developer. Any more introduces unnecessary complexity.

Rapid Publishing

Most of your time should be invested in publishing against a diverse content calendar. The blogging team's goal should be to determine which posts hit a nerve with readers. These most popular themes should dominate the calendar, with more niche topics sprinkled throughout the schedule. The team should write and publish as many posts as possible during this period to gain experience and gather enough reader feedback on the blog's direction and quality.

Rigorous Tracking

Install tracking analytics on your blog before you go live. Google Analytics is free and can be installed with simple cut-and-paste instructions. Don't allow your IT or agency to hold off on installing analytics. It's the first and most important action you can take to ensure success.

Once your blog has been deployed and promoted, shift to the rapid iteration phase.

RAPID TESTING AND ITERATION

Most business blogs fail because their publisher does too little too late. Don't allow your blog to crash against the rocks of neglect and wishful thinking. From the beginning, follow a testing a program that identifies the key success ingredients of content type, traffic sources, and reader behavior.

Content Type

Test a variety of post types to understand which topics resonate with your audience. Judge post success by examining how many times the post is viewed. This metric is called page views and can be easily found in your tracking software. Also pay attention to how many times the post is shared via retweets, LinkedIn shares, and Facebook likes or shares.

Traffic Sources

Evaluate where your blog is getting most of its visitors. At first, in-house sources such as your website and e-mail list will account for most of your traffic. After the first 30 to 60 days, search engines will begin to contribute more traffic.

Pay close attention to the search phrases that contribute the most traffic. Track these search phrases to specific blog posts. Study what parts of the post seemed to trigger search engine rankings. Quickly follow up on any success by writing posts that target well-performing keywords.

Review where your visitors are leaving the blog. Blogs tend to be one-page affairs, meaning that visitors come to read one post and spend little time exploring the blog. Your goal is to get them to stick around and perform an action before leaving. Actions include signing up for blog updates via e-mail or RSS, commenting, or reading other blog posts. Review the "pages per visit" metric in your tracking software to keep an eye on reader actions.

Reader Behavior

Do readers comment on your blog posts? Are they more likely to share posts they like via Twitter, LinkedIn, or Facebook? Business blog posts tend to get more shares versus comments. However, if you want to engage your readers and encourage comments, test different posting styles to see which posts elicit reader reactions. Pay attention to mentions and comments on other social platforms to get a full picture of reader behavior and receptiveness.

Be patient as you dial in your blog's style, voice, and content. Evaluate your performance based on how many experiments you conduct. Get feedback and implement tactics that achieve results.

MINIMUM VIABLE BLOG BLUEPRINT

The following MVB blueprint is a development guide that will cut the time it takes to create and deploy your blog. The core elements of the MVB are open source, easy to implement, and inexpensive to deploy.

Core Blog Software: WordPress

WordPress is the most popular open source blogging software available. You can download it at wordpress.org.

Installation takes about five minutes, and the site offers in-depth tutorials.

Themes

You have two options for designing the creative look of your blog—themes or custom development. For the MVB we recommend you choose a quality premium theme. Some excellent theme design choices include StudioPress, WooThemes, and Themeforest. Select a theme that is suitable to your organization. Don't kill yourself here. Pick something professional and easy to modify.

WordPress Plugins

Plugins are WordPress extensions that add functionality to your blog. There are thousands of plugins available. Here are several key plugins to install immediately:

- Google Analyticator: Installs Google Analytics on your WordPress plugin.
- SEO for WordPress: Configures your blog appropriately for the search engines. This powerful plugin simplifies optimizing your blog for search engine listings.
- Recent/popular posts: Many themes come with a plug-in that stylishly displays recent or popular posts.
- Social sharing plugin: Sharing icons make it easy for your readers to tell their social networks about your posts. Use plugins like the Buffer app to easily configure and place your share icons under your post titles, sidebars, and post footers.

Layout

Use a two-column layout that puts your blog post content in one column and sidebar in the other column. Two-column layouts emphasize your blog post, giving you plenty of room for a prominent headline and photos.

Navigation

Your business blog should be integrated into your main website. This integration has important SEO benefits. In general, search engines value websites that have frequently updated and tightly targeted content. Your blog fits both of these criteria, and your main website will benefit from the integration. In addition, your blog will benefit from being part of an indexed website. This means that your blog posts will be listed and begin attracting search engine traffic faster.

Since your blog is part of the main website, its navigation will have to pull double duty: connect readers with interesting blog content and keep important links from your main website front and center. Combining these two tasks is a balancing act between serving the reader's needs while ensuring that you drive traffic to important parts of your website.

The best approach is to limit the number of links in your navigation. Only include links that are critical to the navigation of the blog and website. Cluttering your navigation areas will only confuse your readers and hurt the performance of the blog.

Sidebar

Blog sidebars often get cluttered with a miscellaneous assortment of gee-whiz blogging gadgets. Your sidebar's job is to get visitors to join your community and visit other pages on your blog. For sidebars, less is definitely more. Start your sidebar with the following:

- **E-mail opt-in form for blog post updates.** Give your readers an option to subscribe to your blog and receive updates via e-mail when a new post is published.
- **Introduce the bloggers.** A blog is an ideal format to put a face to your company. The sidebar is an ideal place to introduce *who* is doing the blogging—and stick a friendly photo up there too. If you are using multiple bloggers, you might include a separate page of bloggers and their bios.
- **Popular posts.** Provide links to the most popular posts on your blog. If your blog is new, offer links to 5 to 10 evergreen posts. Check your blog plugin for an option to display a thumbnail image with each post title.
- **Social icons.** Use your blog to grow your audiences on complementary social platforms. Social sites like Twitter and Facebook offer icons that add readers to your audience with one click. Quickly add new followers by adding a sentence that tells your audience the benefits of connecting with you on other platforms.
- **Helpful services.** Your blog is valuable real estate! It's likely that high-potential prospects will be visiting your blog every day. Why not introduce them to some of your useful services and products in a gentle way? There are several free WordPress plugins you can use to generate helpful ads as a call to action.

That's it for the sidebar. Limiting your sidebar items increases engagement with each item.

LAUNCHING YOUR MVB

First launch your MVB within your own organization. Be prepared to explain the process of rapid testing and evolution of your blog content. Help stakeholders understand the blog's role in the company's communication strategy.

Keeping your blog filled with interesting and relevant content is a team activity. However, adding too many writers too quickly can jeopardize blog post quality and create a logistical bottleneck. Instead, create a process that identifies potential contributors and trains them on blog writing best practices. Add these new authors slowly to ensure that you maintain quality and reduce administrative overhead.

Sit down and discuss the concept of the five core blogging skills and why everyone has the tools to blog effectively. Distribute the Born to Blog Skills Quiz from Chapter 9 to your team to get a quick read on everyone's writing preference.

It's a good idea to set up your MVB with a full roster of posts to help people visualize the look and feel of the blog.

Your blog's success depends on strong and vocal sponsorship from your business's leadership team. From the start, everyone should agree that the blog is intended to build relationships with prospects and customers.

Most of all, demystify the blogging process. Reassure everyone that the blog's success depends on being authentic, conversational, and passionate about the organization's goal.

Once your internal house is in order, move to publicly soft-launching the MVB.

MVB Soft Launch

Start with promoting your blog on your website home page. This is a great place to find readers because visitors are already there to research your products and services.

After your website, start promoting individual blog posts on Twitter, LinkedIn, Facebook, and other social platforms. Be careful to share quality resources before promoting your own posts. Many successful bloggers prefer to share 10 to 12 third-party resources and links for every time they promote their own blog posts. This best practice demonstrates your desire to be helpful first.

The Importance of "Social Proof"

Have you ever walked into a restaurant that was completely empty and felt that maybe you made a mistake coming there? By contrast, a busy, lively restaurant makes us feel like we made a good decision and joined in what is obviously a popular place.

In the absence of real data or truth, we use these environmental clues to help us make decisions. In real life, "social proof" is the trappings of society that impart influence. A person's height, a fancy car, a diploma—all help determine influence, subconsciously. Since we don't have those physical clues in the online world, we look to "badges" like Twitter followers and Facebook "likes" to provide a shortcut assessment. With the density of information in today's world, these badges are very important.

Visiting an empty blog is like walking into an empty restaurant. You just feel uneasy if there is no evidence that anyone else has been there. So having a plan to "prime the pump" and build some social proof is important for a new blog.

> **MARK:** One example I use in my classes is a company with several hundred thousand employees and 90 people working on the blog. Yet most of their blog posts have fewer than two tweets or Facebook likes and no comments. Even if only the internal

bloggers tweeted the post and supported each other with comments, a great deal of social proof would be generated. In this example, the company is sending the message, "Even we don't care about this blog."

To get momentum for your blog, don't be afraid to ask friends and coworkers to help spread the word and build enthusiasm and dialogue on the blog. Creating a community takes patience and time, but contributing to the aspect of social proof can help get you off to a great start.

Setting up your MVB is an important first step. The process is invaluable for securing leadership support, setting team expectations, and creating momentum. With your MVB in place, it's time to focus on the biggest blogging challenge and opportunity—content.

CHAPTER 13

Unlocking Content

It's true. Content is king on the social web. It is the catalyst that makes things happen and ultimately creates business benefits.

Your blog requires a steady supply of excellent content to thrive and survive. This can become a burden if you don't have a game plan for creating the right blend of content for your business blog. Your content should attract new visitors, establish rapport with your readers, educate readers on your approach, and establish your expertise and leadership.

This chapter will provide detailed guidelines on the type of content to offer your readers. But content doesn't always have to be original. Your company is probably a content-producing machine. Sales presentations, speeches, marketing brochures, customer stories, testimonials, training programs—all of these aspects of the everyday life of a company can be a rich source of blog content. Get the most bang for your buck by reusing these content sources on the blog as much as possible!

There isn't one type of silver-bullet content that can accomplish every company goal. Instead, you need to master four types of content: evergreen, identity, people, and bread and butter (B&B) content. We'll discuss each now.

EVERGREEN CONTENT

Evergreen content is always relevant and useful. This content often answers your customers' most common questions. The content rarely is out-of-date because it addresses core issues. For example, a "Mommy Jogger" blog would feature evergreen content that describes the correct use of jogging strollers. This post would be relevant for years.

Your blog will need a full toolbox of evergreen content. This content will get ranked by the search engines and bring in new visitors. Consistently adding new content will broaden the number of search engine terms you can target. Well-written evergreen content has a greater chance of achieving and retaining a first-page search ranking because of its relevance and comprehensive review of the subject.

Evergreen content is versatile and can be repurposed to create new information offerings for your customers. For example, a series of evergreen posts can be compiled, edited, and offered as an in-depth special report on a subject. You can also turn the evergreen posts into slideshows, videos, and e-mail courses.

How to Create Evergreen Content

Focus your efforts initially to create at least 12 evergreen content posts for your blog. Publish these posts evenly throughout the year. Twelve isn't a magic number—it is just a good goal that can be scheduled on a monthly basis.

Examine your customers' most frequently asked questions to select suitable evergreen post subjects. A florist could create a post on how to keep roses fresh for more than a week. A septic tank cleaning service could publish a post on how to avoid common septic tank maintenance issues. The goal is to offer a growing library of easy-to-understand information that attracts new visitors and encourages repeat visits.

Search engine keyword research is another way to uncover good candidates for evergreen posts. Google offers a free keyword tool that will show how many visitors searched for a specific term over a 30-day period. Google's tool also offers suggested keywords based on watching other people's search behavior. These suggestions often offer invaluable insights into actual customer search behavior.

You will be ready to draft evergreen content topics after you've compiled common customer questions and reviewed keyword options. Turn your list of questions and keywords into post headlines. Brainstorm ideas until you've exhausted your list. From here, create a short list of 12 posts that will have a long "shelf life" and attract a healthy number of visitors from search engines.

These evergreen posts form your blog's foundation. Once these posts are in place, you can move on to identity content, a special class of posts designed to build rapport with your visitors.

IDENTITY CONTENT

Your blog visitors will want to know who you are and what your business believes in. Specifically, your customers are looking for reasons to trust you. They want to know if you care about their problems, respect them as people, and care about being a responsive and responsible brand. This is the "identity content" that introduces your business to customers, prospects, suppliers, and investors.

Identity content should explain your company's values and standards. What is the "true north" for your business, and how does it guide your decision making? This content should be clear, compelling, and authentic. You want to give your readers enough information to answer the question, "Do I like these folks?"

Some people insist that this "soft" stuff isn't important. Does P&G really have to talk about its values when I just need a cheap tube of toothpaste? Yes, and it does so. Think of identity content as the blueprint for communicating with readers. It's your manifesto.

A great practical example of this comes from Johnson & Johnson, a company with a fanatical approach to safety and integrity. A few years ago the company took the unusual and unpopular position of suing the American Red Cross. To many, this seemed inconsistent with J&J's values. So to explain the issue, J&J took to its blog and created a brilliant post entitled "You Did What?" that allowed the company to explain the situation and reinforce its core values.

How to Create Identity Content

There isn't a simple formula for identity content because your organization is unique. Your values have been shaped by experience, setbacks, and triumphs. Your identity content should touch on these areas. For example, an advertising agency should craft identity content that expresses its deep reverence for the creative process. A clothing retailer can talk about its commitment to buying clothing from factories that respect the dignity of their workers.

Use identity content to explain policies that guide your decision-making process. Identify the policies that your customers may encounter and explain the reasoning behind them. What is your return policy, and why is it fair? What are your hiring practices, and how do they define your organization? It's likely that this process will reveal policies that are out of line with your core values. This is the time to clarify them and add emotional impact to your communications.

Behind the MacMillan residence hall at Miami University in Oxford, Ohio, there is an ornate sundial donated by the Delta Delta Delta sorority. Spend a moment watching the sundial, and you'll see students reach out and rub the heads of the metal turtles that surround the base of the sundial. Tradition promises good luck to any students who rub the turtles' heads on the way to their exams.

Your identity content will become the turtleheads for your blog writing team. Writing this identity content will instill a sense of purpose. Future blog posts that reference the values of your business can link back to these identity posts.

Usually a blog just needs an occasional, well-written identity post to capture values, policies, and standards. Identity posts should be written and published when you start your business blog and at important company milestones. Perhaps a news event would trigger an opportunity for an identity post. They serve as an inspirational momentum builder that will power your ongoing effort to create an effective blog that enriches your readers' lives.

Ideally, the CEO should write this post. The CEO's contribution will add credibility to your blog and help gain support for the blog within the organization.

PEOPLE CONTENT

Remember that people are attracted to people, not to abstract principles, sound bites, or sanitized corporate communications. We all are drawn to stories that underpin our human experience.

Your business is a community of individuals working toward a common goal. Everyone has families, hobbies, passions, and goals. People content introduces your readers to your employees, the ones that make things happen. Let your readers know that your business isn't just words on a page but people just like them.

People content demonstrates your company culture, highlights milestone events, and gives a glimpse into the lives of your team. Businesses tend to struggle with people content because they are trained to focus on the product or service. Some businesses would rather remain silent than let their employees speak on behalf of the company. This is shortsighted. If you trust your people to deliver a service or manufacture a product, you should be able to empower them to speak for the business. Each employee has the skills needed to blog. Give them the training and the tools to do so.

How to Create People Content

There are plenty of opportunities to write great people content. Let interns draft a post about what they've learned. Ask new employees to talk about your company culture after a year on the team. Create a photo slide show of the company picnic. Document a product brainstorming session. Let your retail personnel talk about memorable customer moments when they were able to satisfy and enrich a customer's life. Introduce new hires and talk about why their position is important for fulfilling your company's mission.

You'll discover that people content will inspire your team to contribute content to the blog. Accept all content, review it, and publish it if it meets your quality guidelines. Keep an eye out for employees who are strong in one of the five core skill sets of dreaming, storytelling, persuading, curating, and teaching.

Try to feature people content at least 10 percent of the time as a goal.

BREAD AND BUTTER CONTENT

Bread and butter (B&B) content will fill most of your editorial calendar. B&B content is short, targeted, and timely. This content is meant to snag the attention of members of your target audience and pull them into your blog.

B&B content can be serious, funny, heartfelt, topical, instructional, or zany. The only rule is that it can't be boring! You don't have to be hilarious, but you have to present your material in an interesting and engaging way.

Plan on filling 80 percent of your editorial schedule with B&B posts. Your subjects should focus on educational topics that introduce your audience to your products or service approach. You want your readers to finish a post and say, "I would like to hear more about product X."

How to Create Bread and Butter Content

B&B content categories include the following:

1. Instructional. Teach your audience how to get the most out of your product. Use your blog to give readers an "insider's tour" of your product's most useful features. Show innovative ways other customers are using the product. View your blog as a supplementary owner's manual filled with fascinating "did you know" content. Customers love to hear stories that will save them time, save them money, or make their lives easier!

The Buffer app is an ingenious tool for scheduling tweets. It's easy to use and has multiple uses. The creators of the Buffer application used their blog as an instructional community-building platform from the beginning. Leo Widrich, a cofounder and community chief, regularly posts content that shares fascinating new ways to use the Buffer app.

The Buffer team also contacts other blogs and offers to write custom B&B content for their bloggers. Of course, the post includes a helpful tidbit about the Buffer app.

When developing this type of content, why not engage blog readers with firsthand knowledge of the product's features?

2. Diagnostic. Help your readers decide if they need to purchase your product. Be the first one to give customers the buying criteria for their purchase. For example, career coaches can write B&B content that helps executives diagnose a potential problem with delegation. If the diagnostic is even-handed and informative, readers are likely to select your services when they have a need.

Diagnostic B&B content includes checklists, tests and quizzes, and case studies. Case studies are effective because they are practical demonstrations of your product solving someone's problem. It's simpler for customers to imagine themselves using the product to solve their problem.

Marketing, sales, and customer service are the best choice for producing this content. Diagnostic content is a more comprehensive type of in-person "framing the problem" interviews. The sales team conducts these types of interviews with prospects every day. Get them to identify the best questions and turn them into an engaging post that invites the reader to walk through the process.

Remember that blogs are considered to be commercially neutral platforms. While readers will tolerate sales pitches, they expect to receive a good deal of free relationship-building content first. Giving away excellent information is the best way to quickly turn your blog into a platform for direct sales.

3. Proof. Lewis Howes is widely recognized as being an expert LinkedIn consultant. He teaches his LinkedIn methods in high-octane webinars where hundreds of people attend to hear his insights. At the start of the webinar, Lewis promises listeners that they will be able to put his methods into action for themselves. Next he walks everyone through a step-by-step method for getting a top listing on LinkedIn.

Many listeners are skeptical, but in 15 minutes, impromptu praise starts flooding in. Webinar participants begin expressing their delight at getting a top listing using Lewis's methods. At this point, Lewis can sell them anything. But he holds off and delivers another 45 minutes of useful "proof" content. At the end, he makes an attractive offer that is snapped up by the audience. It's a no-brainer because everyone has already seen proof of Lewis's expertise.

Proof posts are surgically precise and immediately compelling. Your readers are searching for proof of your expertise. These posts deliver. The best proof posts lead the reader through a step-by-step process that is focused on solving a single problem. This isn't teaser content—it is an exhaustive guide. The reader finishes the post overwhelmed by your willingness to offer quantifiable value.

Proof posts are different from instructional posts because they are directed at prospective customers. These prospects are in the prebuy stage and are looking for reasons to include or eliminate you from their short list.

Writing proof posts can be divided into three parts:

1. **Describe the problem and promise a solution.**
   Pinpoint an annoying customer problem that costs
   your readers considerable time and money. Preferably,
   pick a problem that your product is particularly well
   suited to solve. Spend a paragraph concretely describing the problem.
2. **Solve the problem.** Don't hold back. Walk through
   detailed steps complete with supporting photos, illustrations, or screenshots. Your goal is to "shock and
   awe" the reader with your willingness to give away
   valuable information. Your solution to the problem will convince the reader you have expertise and
   experience.
3. **Keep your foot in the door.** Let your readers know
   that you have more advice and information to offer.
   Invite them to return to your blog to get more.
   Encourage them to comment on the material and
   how they plan to use the information.

That's it. Three parts and you are done with the post.
Stay on the lookout for opportunities to share new methods,
recommendations, and ideas with your audience. Overload
them with incredible information that gives them a preview
of how you would interact with them as a customer.

OK, now that we have our content plan in place, how do
we get people to read it?

CHAPTER 14

Attracting Readers

As we discussed, there are many benefits to blogging. It can greatly enhance your search traffic, provide PR opportunities, and help define your thought leadership. But let's face it. You want somebody to read the darn thing, too. Readers are the lifeblood of a blog.

You are better off setting the goal of growing your blog right from the beginning. There are hundreds of techniques for attracting readers to your blog. A Google search will serve up millions of sites clamoring to share the latest blog promotion tip. But few of these tips start with the right objective.

Before you start attracting readers, commit to finding the *right kind of reader.*

For business blogs, the "right" reader is usually a potential customer with disposable income and a desire to solve a problem. Of course, there are many important secondary audiences too—the public at large, people who love you, people who hate you, suppliers, even competitors. However, over time, blogs should be aimed at creating shareholder value, and the most powerful way to do this is to attract and serve customers.

If your blog is filled with self-serving press releases, rehashed product announcements, and award mentions, then you are talking to someone other than your customer. This is one reason we tend to favor the idea of a business blog being "owned" by the marketing department.

Obviously, the contributors can come from all corners of the company, but at least the strategy should be owned by marketing since in the end we view blogs as being a customer acquisition and service platform, no matter the size of your organization.

From this point forward, assume that when we say "readers," we're primarily referring to people who are willing to buy what you're selling.

This chapter describes eight easy ways to attract loyal readers.

1. GIVE AWAY YOUR BEST

Set the goal of giving away the best information possible to your blog readers. For many readers, your blog will be their first introduction to your company. Make sure they know that you value their time and are committed to helping them learn all they can about your products and mission.

Your openness will encourage your readers to share this content with their audience. Make sure to include the address of your blog prominently on the homepage and in page footers. Your free, high-quality content will bring new readers to your blog for years.

> **MARK:** Many people in service industries will be puzzled by this advice—give away your best stuff. If you give it away, what do you have left to sell?
>
> Every day on my blog, I give away tips for social media marketing, and in fact, if you read and retained everything I have written, you probably wouldn't have to hire me. And yet, people do. In fact, my blog has represented my entire business marketing effort. At least 90 percent of my sales leads are "inbound"

leads with no selling expense, no RFQs to fill out, no sales pitches. Prospects are attracted to my blog because I demonstrate my knowledge, my philosophy, and my trustworthiness with every post I write.

Even if you think you are giving away the good stuff, customers still need you to teach them, coach them, and provide your expertise for their specific problems. Giving away knowledge may sound crazy, but it is smart business because it works.

One of my blog readers, Tony Dowling, took this advice seriously and created a blog called "Completely Free Marketing Advice." The Welsh entrepreneur decided that instead of selling so hard, he was going to build his reputation by building a blog community and helping others. In his own words, this strategy "transformed" his business and changed his life.

2. ADD YOUR BLOG TO CURRENT MARKETING EFFORTS

Look for opportunities to place your blog address on current outbound advertising and communications. Anything is fair game for a blog address including business cards, letterhead, invoices, publications, and PowerPoint presentations. Promote your blog anywhere you have your e-mail address

3. CONTRIBUTE TO OTHER PUBLICATIONS

Find where your audience currently gets information about your product. In the B2B world, prospects are likely to review industry-specific sites, blogs, and professional publications. Contributing articles, columns, and posts to those publications is the most effective way to attract them to your website. In social media circles, this is called guest posting, and it's still a proven traffic generator. It's not unusual for a guest post on Mark's site to get 300-400 visits back to the author's home site.

4. GET ACTIVE ON YOUR READER'S SOCIAL CHANNELS

Many readers are spending increasing amounts of time on social platforms that cater to their tastes. Business professionals roam LinkedIn; artists, illustrators, and crafters are on Pinterest. Journalists, subject matter experts, and early adopters prefer Twitter and Google+. With over a billion members, everybody else is on Facebook!

Spend some time researching where your audience likes to spend time getting information about your subject. Do a keyword searches on LinkedIn and Facebook to get a list of groups and Facebook pages focused on your niche. Visit these areas and check out the activity level. Look for groups where members are offering quality information and answering questions. Use tools like Twellow.com and Wefollow. com to search for your industry by keyword to get a list of influencers and assess how many people are using Twitter to get information about your niche. A powerful platform like Appinions.com can unearth significant new venues and audiences for your content.

Focus your attention on the most active platforms first. Experiment to see what types of messages attract people to your blog. Resist the urge to spread yourself thin by being active on dozens of social platforms at once.

5. USE SAVVY, SIMPLE SEO

Search engine optimization (SEO) is an important technique for getting targeted readers to visit your blog. SEO is the process of making tweaks to your blog posts to help search engines rank them highly. A first-page listing on Google can bring hundreds of visitors per day depending on the keyword.

SEO is a sophisticated skill set requiring in-depth study and experimentation to master. That's why we advocate understanding the fundamentals and doing the minimum required to show up on the search engine's radar screen. It's a complicated and dynamic field but a few basic SEO actions include:

- **Research and compile a list of keywords.** Keywords are the terms your readers would use to find information about your topic. Imagine them typing these words into a search engine whenever they have a question. Google offers a keyword tool that helps you pinpoint the words your readers would likely use. Also, look at your Google Analytics. This will show you what keywords people are already using to find you. Compile a list of these words and keep them nearby for reference.
- **Optimize your blog title.** Google hunts for web pages and blog posts that have relevant information for its users. Google's indexing algorithm looks for clues that your page is the right match for the user. One important clue (or signal) is detecting the searcher's keyword in the title of your blog post. When appropriate, include a keyword from your research list in the title of your post. Don't overdo it! Only include the keyword if it makes sense and doesn't hurt the meaning for human readers.
- **Optimize post content.** Google and other search engines also scan your post's content looking for

keywords that are relevant to the searcher's request. Look for opportunities to weave your targeted keyword into the post's content.

Again, remember to write for human beings first. Only include a keyword if it will not hurt the readability of the text. Your goal is to offer discreet assistance to the search engines. Also understand that Google is the most sophisticated search engine on the planet. It will detect "over optimization" and penalize your blog with lower search listings or even ban your blog from the index. This is easy to avoid if you write great content first and optimize your text where it makes sense.

We could write another book on this topic alone, but optimizing your keywords, blog titles, and content is an excellent first start. If you want to explore this topic in depth, we recommend Lee Odden's book *Optimize*.

6. HOST GUEST BLOGGERS

Once you have your blog up and running, why not consider opening the door to external guest posts? When done correctly, hosting guest bloggers is a win-win for you and the blog writer. If your blog is steadily increasing its exposure and popularity, posting on your blog is a way to expand their audience.

Hosting guest bloggers also lightens your workload while providing new voices and perspectives for your audience. Guest bloggers are reader magnets because the best ones aggressively promote their guest post appearances to their audience, driving new readers to your blog. Think of the power of turning over your blog to customer posts and industry experts! What amazing advocacy that would be, and many companies do this today.

There's only one rule for soliciting and publishing guest posts: Maintain your quality standards! Setting the bar high will demonstrate your commitment to quality and attract talented writers who respect your editorial discipline. On the other hand, accepting questionable posts will drive away readers and attract "junk producers" who only want to exploit your readers.

One best practice is to establish a short list of guest post guidelines that will establish expectations for content, quality, post length, and so on. Also cover ownership of the content and whether it is OK for the post to show up on other blogs.

7. JOIN AND SPONSOR CONVERSATIONS (TWITTER CHATS AND FORUMS)

Right now, people with similar interests are gathering to share information and recommendations. They aren't meeting physically. They are meeting via social channels like Twitter and specialized websites called forums. On Twitter, these gatherings are called Twitter chats. The moderator of the Twitter chat advertises when a chat will start, who will be moderating, and the hashtag for tracking the chat. This is an exceptional way to find people who might be interested in you and your blog.

Discussion Forums

While not as popular as they used to be, forums are still a great spot to find potential readers. Do your research and make sure that you select a discussion forum that is active, cordial, and relevant to your topic. Steer away from forums that aren't moderated or that allow unsponsored advertising. Examples of places with excellent topical forums are Yahoo,

Focus, and Quora. Research from The Social Habit shows that forum and chat room participation is still on par with blog readership.

Once you've found a suitable forum, spend a few weeks being a good citizen by asking and answering questions from fellow forum participants. Follow the rules closely and look for influential participants. These influencers might publish blogs that accept guest posts or might submit a guest post for your blog.

8. REWARD YOUR READERS

There are no shortcuts to building a community. You have to connect to one reader at a time. Once readers start coming onto your blog and commenting, find ways to reward them by leaving a return comment, visiting their blog, and looking for ways to encourage them to come back.

Success on the social web comes from many small interactions that lead to bigger interactions, which lead to relationships. A blog can be a very powerful part of this formula, providing opportunities for lots of these small interactions. It's usually a small step between being a loyal blog reader and becoming a loyal customer.

Piece by piece, we're putting together a great blogging strategy. We have a plan, content, and ideas to promote it. Now let's really get this thing rocking by turning your employees on to blogging.

CHAPTER 15

Attracting and Nurturing Blog Contributors

A T&T, the technology and communications giant, had a problem. How would it move its venerable brand into the digital age and connect with customers on the social web? The answer, the company found, was through its passionate employees.

A key element of the company's transformation has been deputizing employees to lead the charge. In 2011, AT&T introduced the idea of a "business network" of company bloggers writing about all the things that they loved best—technology, customers, service. This type of firsthand experience and expertise simply couldn't come from an ad agency or PR department. It had to come from the people who were actually touching the customers every day.

The marketing department provided training and support to a handful of early enthusiasts. The company also salted in some professional writers to demonstrate best blogging practices and provided coaching in the early stages. The experiment turned into a movement, and month by month, dozens of new bloggers joined in, eager to share their stories and educate customers on valuable technology tips.

Slowly, companies are realizing that their best evangelists, storytellers, and teachers aren't housed in an advertising agency or PR firm. Many companies are insisting that social media and blogging competency be homegrown rather than outsourced to Madison Avenue. With this approach comes the need to quickly find and train blog contributors from every corner of the company.

WHERE TO START YOUR SEARCH

Here are some ideas on where to find blogging talent within your company.

Customer Service

Customer service representatives have learned how to anticipate and solve customer issues. They are belly to belly with irate and delighted customers alike and are passionate customer advocates! Sounds like the perfect blogger!

These shock troops often have the real-world expertise needed to pick blog topics that help customers most. Approach the head of customer service and ask him or her to point out the most effective customer service representatives. Interview them for blogging topics. Keep an eye out for representatives that want to help customers in new ways.

Retail Staff

Pinpoint the best-performing retail locations and buy the managers lunch. Pick their brain about how they run their stores and their philosophy for taking care of customers and clients. Look for customer success stories that demonstrate your company's core competencies and service values. Would the customers be willing to contribute? Find ways to celebrate amazing employees.

Product-Engineering

Customers and clients love to hear the story behind the product. They like to know that real people are focused on solving their problems. They can't help but cheer and celebrate the eureka moment. Look to companies like Apple that regularly highlight their top executives in videos describing the passion and vision behind their products.

The C-Suite

Count yourself lucky if you have a blogging CEO. Your CEO has the most credibility with customers, prospects, and the general public. The CEO is the steward of the company's vision and values. By all means, work to get your CEO excited about blogging. Point him or her to Michael Dell (Dell Computers), Bill Marriott (Marriott Hotels), and Tony Hsieh (Zappos) as examples of crazy-busy executives who invest time in blogging.

If your CEO can't or won't blog, then start canvasing the C-suite. The chief marketing officer should be blogging—no excuses. Other potential candidates include the chief operating officer, sales, product engineering, and strategy. When you make your pitch, be sure to mention that you have an easy template and only need 600 words. Offer to ghostwrite from an outline or work with the executive to edit the submission before publishing.

Marketing and PR

Your marketing team will likely be the primary contributors to the business blog. These folks are often superb storytellers and enjoy finding ways to connect the dots for customers.

Other Sources

We have seen some amazing blogs created by a company's customers, suppliers, community members, and other stakeholders. Examples might be:

- A community member blogging about how your company is a good corporate neighbor to mark a company anniversary or milestone.
- A supplier blogging about a new cooperative practice that will result in new benefits for end customers.
- One of the best blog posts we have ever seen was written by a person retiring after 30 years with the same company. The employee insisted on saying "goodbye" to all his customers in a very homespun and emotional farewell. Wow. What an impact!

HOW CAN YOU SPOT A STAR BLOG CONTRIBUTOR?

It helps to start with the right mindset. As we discussed, anyone has the raw materials to be a great blogger. But the real differentiator can be enthusiasm. If you have somebody who is driven to help, that is an incredible building block for success. This person is likely willing to learn, grow, and keep improving. Starting out, enthusiasm and commitment are probably more important than stellar writing skills.

We believe that anybody has the potential to be a blogging star. Yes, even *you* were "Born to Blog." You and your employees have the innate skills. But you might need a little coaching.

BLOGGER COACHING

Now that you have identified your team, be prepared for disappointment. You know all those people who said they would help you? They probably won't! Let's face the facts of company life—priorities can change when the rubber meets the road, and people need to start delivering content on deadlines.

In the face of bureaucracy, employee turnover, legal constraints, and shifting priorities, a best practice is to have a central coordinator or editor who also serves as the leader of the content plan and a blogger development coach. This can be a big job, and if you do not want to add to overhead, it is possible to contract this function out successfully to an experienced blogger. We have seen this trend at many companies, especially until they hit critical mass and can justify an internal position.

An extremely important part of this coordinator position is ongoing coaching for the team of bloggers. With the expectation for high quality, there simply must be a consistent editorial expectation and training so bloggers become more and more competent and self-sufficient over time.

Remember that this coach is not just building a blog; he or she is building an engaged team of volunteers. So we need to keep organizational considerations in mind as well as practical content development needs.

Once bloggers have submitted their posts, take the time to offer comprehensive and helpful advice. Resist the urge to "ding" posts that conflict with your sense of style. Remember that your readers aren't cut from a homogenous mold. They have different tastes, outlooks, and priorities. The best way to connect with them is by publishing a diverse mix of quality posts in differing styles. Build competencies slowly through both formal training and in-the-moment coaching opportunities.

Any blog coaching should include these functions:

Specific Blog-Writing Skills and Quality Expectations

- Headlines should be simple, benefit oriented, and interesting.
- Lead paragraphs should be enticing and thought provoking.
- The post body should have an appropriate topic and length and be jargon-free and simple to understand.
- Editing skills should be polished, and posts should be proofread twice before submission.
- Posts should be concise: straight to the point and word-stingy.
- Calls to action should be included in posts as appropriate.
- Writing time-savers should be used and shared. For example, writing several posts at one time while you are inspired or have time will help during periods when there you have little time to write. Encourage the cross-pollination of best practices.
- Blog writers should be encouraged to contribute ideas to a content plan.

Community Management

- How do we handle comments?
- What happens if controversy erupts?
- Legal considerations (especially in regulated industries).

Community Building

- Developing basic social networking skills
- Helping to create an audience for the company blog
- Igniting the content and social proof

Over time, other team members can add their expertise and experience to the training.

As AT&T developed its team of more than 100 internal bloggers, it offered a wide range of support activities to build this competency:

- Formal training meetings
- Access to an editor/coach
- Contests to reward improvement
- Topical live and recorded workshops
- Monthly "office hours" to discuss company blog problems and opportunities
- Consistent personal coaching from an outside professional

While the company made a concerted effort to attract bloggers at first, the natural enthusiasm of the team attracted more people interested in blogging from nearly every functional corner of the company.

The company also featured guest posts from industry experts and other stakeholders and, after an initial start-up period, began to focus on more advanced skills like community building and blog promotion. The company has a dashboard to share progress and celebrate milestones. It even has an annual live award ceremony to recognize the most improved bloggers!

Although this is an example from a large company, the same principles of inclusion, coaching, support, and continuous improvement can be duplicated at any company.

For AT&T and many other companies, the blog is an increasingly important marketing tool. Companies are also finding ways to monetize their efforts directly and indirectly. Let's look at some of the best practices next.

CHAPTER 16

Making Your Blog Pay

Ana never thought of herself as tech-savvy entrepreneur. She just loved swinging a hammer and had a knack for simplifying complex woodworking projects. She spent her time honing her craft in her workshop in Alaska—waiting out the infamously cold winters by creating new designs.

While searching for a way to share her woodworking plans, Ana discovered Blogger, Google's free blogging software. In 2009, Blogger was the best way to start a blog with minimal technical skills.

Ana's plan was simple: post a new woodworking design every day. As a mom, she didn't have time for a complicated blogging strategy. She created simple plans, posted them, and continued with her regular routine.

In just a year, Ana had posted over 400 plans offering guidance on building everything from loft beds to chicken coops. Her growing audience loved Ana's eye for quality and elegant simplicity. They offered encouragement, feedback, and pictures of their own completed projects from Ana's plans.

As word spread, Ana's blog cruised past the one million page views milestone in just three months!

It didn't stop there. Every month she registered another one million page views. The chatter around her plans soon caught the attention of Black & Decker, Sherwin-Williams, and other "do-it-yourself" brands.

Adding the popular photo-sharing service Pinterest to the mix helped accelerate her blog's success. Now this stay-at-home mom earns enough from advertising on her blog to completely support her family.

Ana's story isn't unique. She represents a growing number of people who are turning hobbies and ideas into blog-based businesses. Since blogs are cheap (even free) to set up, they are attractive tools for rapidly testing new business ideas and getting valuable information about what consumers want and the information they need to make a decision.

FOUR WAYS TO TURN READERS INTO CUSTOMERS

Strategies for turning blog readers into customers (or monetizing your audience) can be grouped into four models:

Advertising

Selling access to your audience is the simplest monetization model for most blogs. Advertising options include pay-per-click and CPM (cost per thousand impressions)

The pay-per-click model popularized by Google Adsense can be set up via Google in just a few steps. Bloggers set up an area on their blog's home page dedicated to running ads, and advertisers pay based on the number of banner clicks or number of times their ad has been shown.

The cost per impression model is slightly more complicated but relatively easy to implement. This model usually requires registering with an ad network. An ad network's job is to attract advertisers and connect them with websites and blogs that offer advertising space. The ad network charges the advertisers a fee based on CPM or cost per thousand impressions. So a $25 CPM would earn the blogger $25 for every thousand views/impressions of the ad.

While advertising is simple to set up, it's difficult for bloggers to earn significant revenue unless their blog attracts tens of thousands of visitors per day. Also be aware that blogs have a strong tradition of being advertising-free zones where readers can get their information without being pestered by commercial appeals. This sentiment varies by blogger.

If your goal is to keep commercial transactions at arm's length, then a pure advertising relationship is the best option. While this choice requires a daily flow of high-quality content, it does create a bright line between the business side and the editorial content.

Affiliate Products

Many retailers offer an affiliate program that pays a commission to websites that promote their products. Amazon is the most recognized retailer that offers this affiliate arrangement. The retailer provides a trackable link that is included in blog posts or dedicated ads. When someone purchases a product using the link, the retailer logs the sale and pays the blogger a commission.

The commission structure depends on the retailer and market demand. For example, retailers offering digital information products such as e-books or online training often pay their affiliates 50 to 75 percent commissions. Physical product retailers often pay much lower commissions reflecting the razor-thin profit margins in their markets.

Promoting affiliate products is an effective way to start making money with a blog. There are a number of highly regarded affiliate brokers who make it easy to find relevant products to promote. Commission Junction, ShareASale,

PepperJam, and ClickBank are the most popular places to start looking for suitable affiliate products.

Another variation of the affiliate sale is a "promoted post." Some companies approach well-known bloggers and pay them to promote or review their products with a favorable spin. This is treacherous territory. Turning your blog content into advertising space can be profitable but jeopardizes the trust and integrity you have worked so long to establish with your readers.

It's an essential business practice and legal requirement to disclose to your readers when you are promoting an affiliate product or a promoted post. A best practice is to disclose in the copy of the article that you are being compensated for a link, review, or post. Like advertising, it's critical that bloggers associate themselves with products that are relevant to the subject and audience. Selling cats' scratching posts to dog owners is a great way to turn your blog into a ghost town.

Selling Your Own Products

Creating and selling your own products is the most profitable monetization strategy. In this scenario, you keep all of the profits and build a valuable customer list. With your own products, you can sidestep quality and relevancy concerns because your product will be tailor-made to meet your audience's needs. Readers will also trust recommendations for your own product since they have assessed your trustworthiness and expertise through your blog post writing.

Another advantage of this opportunity is that making money is somewhat less dependent on driving huge amounts of traffic to the blog. A core group of enthusiastic fans can be a good base to build a profitable business from your value-added products.

Of course, selling your own product requires you to actually develop your products! This obviously takes time and investment depending on the type of products you offer. Information producers and service providers have an easier time creating products since their initial investment is just time to write the product and possibly contracting graphics or video production.

Indirect Sales

A blog is an incredibly powerful marketing tool that connects your passions and talents to the world. Sometimes, that's enough to make a blog pay off.

> **MARK:** My blog essentially *is* my marketing plan. It connects with people all over the world, and they get to know me as a person and as a professional. They learn about what I stand for, my strengths, and even my weaknesses, I suppose! But I'm selling personal services—professional speaking, publications, marketing consulting, and corporate workshops. This is a very personal decision. You need to know and trust a person you hire for this role, and I've found that the blog is a great way to connect in a very human way with my audience.
>
> I have created nearly all of my business opportunities from my blog. I was hired by a Fortune 500 company because the senior VP of marketing loved my blog. He had never even met me before and hired me without even a phone call. This is an example of the very powerful indirect selling value of a blog.

BLOG MONETIZATION RULES OF THUMB

A blog's strength flows from reader respect and trust. It's easy to violate that trust with ill-timed promotional pitches or excessive advertising. Most corporate blogs really have no aim to monetize anything directly, counting on the blog to create sales leads over time. Monetizing your audience is as much as an art as it is a science. On one hand you create and nurture relationships with readers; on the other hand you must move those same readers closer to making a purchasing decision.

It's helpful to remember the following guidelines while performing this balancing act.

Be Patient

Rushing to monetize your audience can ruin reader trust and stall your blog's growth. Think of your blog as a medium-to long-term revenue option. Initially invest your resources in creating relevant information and building relationships with readers. Convince them that your blog is committed to quality. Invite them to join your e-mail lists, provide feedback through comments, and connect with you on other social platforms. Use the time to earn their trust.

Once you have laid this groundwork of commitment, reliability, and authenticity, then turn your attention to monetizing your reader base. You'll discover that your initial patient investment in nurturing dialogue and trust will turn into excellent financial results.

Mike Stelzner supplied free, high-quality content every day for more than a year on his *Social Media Examiner* blog before even beginning to apply a monetization strategy. He patiently built a huge and enthusiastic audience through his exceptional content. His blog posts are still free, but over time he added options for paid online webinars, workshops, a book, and live events. Within two years, his blog had become a multimillion-dollar enterprise with a staff of full-time employees.

Be Transparent

Tell your readers exactly what you are doing. Don't waste time trying to hide your intention to earn revenue. Your readers already suspect that you need to be compensated for your time and investment. All they want is for you to be honest with them.

Disclose when you are recommending products that pay commissions. Be up-front about your blog's role in building a business or promoting a product. Immediately address any reader concerns about your activities. Of course, there will be people who will object to any commercial activity, but the majority of your readers will welcome your transparency.

Put Value First

Make sure to promote the value of any product or service that you offer. Use plain language to explain exactly what the reader will get by following your recommendation or purchasing your product. Address any potential objections with blog posts that clearly spell out your intentions and the value being offered. Think of your blog as a pre-sell vehicle with the job of assuaging concerns and handling objections.

Be Discreet

Realize that any advertising can diminish reader opinion about your blog. Think through any overt promotion. Tactics such as pop-up advertising and sidebar banner ads can work but may also scare off a significant portion of your audience. It's better to make your recommendations and promotional appeals within the context of a well-considered blog post or personal e-mail to your readers.

Successful bloggers often use a strategy that maximizes relationship building on the front end while targeting marketing messaging to specific readers out of the glare of public attention.

This strategy was adopted from the direct mail industry and offers powerful techniques for blog monetization.

FRONT-END VERSUS BACK-END MONETIZATION STRATEGY

Imagine your blog as having both a public and private side. On the public side, you focus on establishing trust and reinforcing your business's value proposition. These are your "front-end" tactics.

Ultimately, the goal is to get your readers to raise their hands and give you permission to contact them privately, most of the time via e-mail. In exchange for their permission, you agree to offer them exclusive content and access to offers generally not available to the public. You also promise to police your messages to make sure that they aren't "spammed" by frequent, irrelevant e-mail advertising.

Savvy bloggers offer free reports, e-books, and discounted products in exchange for e-mail and physical addresses. Once the reader grants this permission, the blogger switches to "back-end" tactics.

Back-end tactics are focused on creating a customer or increasing the profit on a previous sale. For example, immediately offering a discounted e-book once a person signs up for a free report is a common back-end tactic. Offering an "upsell," such as selling a video course after the customer purchases an e-book is also a common back-end transaction.

A back-end transaction can happen immediately after a reader signs up for an e-mail list or be implemented over months, depending on the business's goals. Successful back-end follow-up allows the business to offer valuable product for minimal cost (even free) since it can make up the loss "on the back end."

The entire front-end/back-end process can be simple. A blog post with a "sign up for updates" call to action with a welcome e-mail recommending an affiliate product is a low-risk, low-cost way to implement the strategy.

Well, all of this might sound pretty good to you by now, but the trek is not always easy. Let's look at some tactics to consider when things start to go wrong.

CHAPTER 17

Rocks in the Road

Unto every blog some rain must fall. Or something like that.

Nearly every company's blogging activity slips into the doldrums at some point. Here are a few of the common pitfalls you are likely to encounter and some practical ideas on dealing with them.

YOUR LAWYER IS WAITING

There is a healthy tension between most marketing and legal departments. Frankly, any group that keeps you out of jail seems pretty swell to us! By and large, lawyers are there to help you. So the key to getting through the legal channels is to have a well-defined process up front. It doesn't really matter what the process is. You're a survivor. You can make it work. Just make sure it is clearly defined at the beginning.

Now, here's a little secret. Lean a little closer to the book so Legal can't hear it. Over time, the legal requirements almost always loosen up. Once the legal team members realize having a blog is not the corporate apocalypse, they kind of relax on things. Heck, they don't want to review the blog any more than you want them to.

DEADLINE, WHAT DEADLINE?

At some point the posting schedule will fall apart if you are relying on volunteer efforts to fuel your blog content. Unless you have truly special persuasive skills, or perhaps some power of blackmail over your fellow bloggers, chances are the energy will sag at some point and people will miss their deadlines.

There is only one surefire way to make sure this doesn't happen. Before you ever start your blog, go up the chain of command to the highest person in the organization *all* the bloggers fall under—no matter what department. It may be a vice president or even the president of the company. You must secure not only this leader's buy-in but his or her active interest. The leader needs to ask questions about the blog at staff meetings so the management team knows this is a priority. If you don't have management understanding and buy-in, you'll probably have to wait to start your blog until you do.

YOU AREN'T GETTING ANY COMMENTS

Many companies have high expectations that a blog will begin a "conversation with the customer." Hopefully this will occur, but it may not happen for a very long time. It is very, very difficult to get people to comment on company blogs compared to personal blogs. Here are a few reasons why:

- Customers may not be permitted to comment on blogs.
- Customers may not have access to the social web during work hours.
- They may prefer not to put anything in writing, instead responding in other ways.

- Most company blogs have multiple bloggers, and it is difficult to form a connection with a tag-team group of bloggers.
- A rule of thumb is that only 2 percent of blog readers become commenters, so you need a lot of readers before you start getting comments!

So you need to manage expectations up front that most likely you *won't* get any comments for maybe a year or more. This is not a cop-out—it's just the way the web works. It may happen sooner, and if you follow the best practices laid out in *Born to Blog* it probably will, but building a community takes time, consistency, and patience.

YOU AREN'T GETTING ANY READERS

If you aren't getting any readers after six to nine months, it may be time to retrench and adjust. Look at four areas:

1. Are you proactively and systematically building your network, using some of the tools in this book? In particular, Twitter can help attract a relevant audience.
2. Is it time to tweak your content strategy? Survey your customers and ask them what they like and don't like about the blog and adjust.
3. Are you effectively promoting the blog? If you have at least a few loyal readers, you must be doing something right. Maybe it's a matter of making an effort to promote the blog.
4. Are you creating social proof (see Chapter 12) to help make readers feel welcome? Get employees, friends, and family members to help tweet and comment to create an atmosphere of "busyness" on the blog.

YOU HAVE RUN OUT OF THINGS TO WRITE ABOUT

Say it ain't so! It can't be possible!

It's not only possible, it's probable that at some point the well of content ideas will run dry. We've already provided many content-generating ideas in the book, but here are four surefire ways to jump-start your creative juices:

1. Google "what do I write about?" Seriously! You will be amazed at how many lists of amazing ideas you will get to help you through writer's block.
2. Go to a LinkedIn group related to your industry. Look through the questions people are asking. Find an interesting topic. Answer it. That is your blog post,
3. Walk down to customer service. Get a list of all the questions customers have. Answer them, one by one, as blog posts.
4. Try a video blog. Heck, you can make a blog-quality video on your smartphone. Ask a customer if it is OK to interview him or her for your blog. Or sit down with a senior executive or another employee with high visibility and shoot a four- to five-minute video. Great content!

YOUR BLOG HAS STRAYED

Your blog probably is much different from what it was six months earlier. Hopefully you are learning, growing, and improving every day.

But maybe it has gone in the wrong direction. Maybe it is moving away from the core company goals and really hasn't found its "voice."

It's logical to think that your audience expects a "buttoned-up" professional tone in your blog posts. This would make sense if you believe that your blog is an advertisement for your business. But you know better than that by now! Your blog is the personable and approachable extension of your brand.

A stilted, precise, professional tone will remind your reader of the one thing they are trying to avoid—an advertisement.

Your "voice" is perhaps the most elusive quality to master. Your blog's author or authors will represent your voice but their writing style will reflect their perspective and approach. That's why the most effective blogs are often authored by business owners and founders.

This doesn't mean that others shouldn't contribute to your blog. It does mean that your team will need to pay careful attention to how each blog post "feels" and create a unifying tone over time.

After six to nine months take a look at your blog.

Is the content still aligned with the original goals? Do the metrics support that?

Is the tone progressing toward becoming more confident, more open, and more helpful?

Do you have a strong blend of the four different types of blog posts, with about 80 percent being "bread and butter" posts that address customer needs?

You don't have to make everybody conform to one tone. People have different writing styles. But the blog overall should have a unifying personality.

MANAGEMENT WANTS TO KNOW THE ROI OF THE BLOG

Of course they do. They are paid to ask that question. And you'd better be able to show the value of the blog, or you will be out on the street.

Here are some basic philosophical maxims to address management concerns.

We Have the Data

It is absolutely possible to measure the value of blogging. What is the leading measurement of PR and advertising? "Impressions." So counting the number of possible views is a well-known leading indicator of brand awareness. We're lucky to have a precise measure of "page views" to provide an even more accurate measure because this is not an estimate of views. It is *actual* views. And together with "time on page" and "bounce rate" (people who leave right away), you have an excellent formula to watch your blog progress over time.

There are also many fantastic technology options to connect content marketing efforts like blogging with your sales funnel. One well-known company for this is HubSpot.

It's More than ROI

Let's say you get this customer comment in a meeting: "I loved your last blog post. In fact, I printed it out and sent it around the office because it solved the exact problem we had been struggling with." Now—what is the ROI of *that*? How do you put that fantastic comment on a pie chart?

The point is that qualitative data are just as valuable, and often more valuable, than quantitative data. Your best return from the blog may be in awareness, reputation, problem solving, and establishing a voice of authority in your industry. That is legitimate business value.

For this reason, small companies often have an advantage over large companies that have inflexible reporting systems. Blogging absolutely can increase sales, but don't overlook the other value!

Track and Communicate

Even if your management is not asking you to measure, do it anyway. Do not get lulled into a false sense of security, because at some point, the management team is going to bring in some steely-eyed outside consultant to slash overhead. On that day, the consultant is going to sit across a desk from you and, after exchanging some pleasantries about the weather, will uncoil like a striking cobra and ask this question: "Now, why exactly are we doing this blog?"

And that's when you pull out the spreadsheet you have been keeping diligently and communicating to management every month. This spreadsheet is the equivalent of a lightsaber, which you will use to behead the cobra because it clearly shows, month by month, how the blog has been increasingly, and specifically, contributing to company goals. Always keep this lightsaber by your side. For most blogs, there are three important goals:

1. Traffic goals: How many people visit the blog, and especially how many people *revisit* the blog.
2. Activity goals: What are people doing on the blog, and does their activity move them closer to a specific action.
3. Conversion goals: What do people do after being exposed to the blog.

May the Force be with you.

CHAPTER 18

Getting Personal

*A lot of presidential memoirs, they say, are dull and self-serving.
I hope mine is interesting and self-serving.*

President Bill Clinton

Memoirs were the personal coda for statesmen, businesspeople, and military leaders, an exhaustive recollection of their insights on critical events that shaped their lives. Often writing a memoir was a defensive measure to ensure that history got the story right.

Everyday people didn't get book deals for their memoirs. Instead, every evening they retired to their bedrooms, dens, or front porches and described their day in a diary. Their entries could be a cursory inventory of farming suppliers or brutal self-examination. Historians prize these town folk diaries for their unvarnished reflection of daily events.

While diaries are still kept (and stolen) and memoirs are still published, the blog has assumed the role of the modern memoir.

Technorati's annual "State of the Blogosphere" reports that 61 percent of blogs are written by hobbyists. These hobby bloggers are passionate about an interest, and they can't help but tell the world about it. Their blogs are a labor of love with 60 percent of respondents noting that they write for "personal satisfaction" and not monetary gain.

This section of the book is for you.

> **STANFORD:** Reading personal blogs is an introspective and intimate experience. While researching this book, I read gut-wrenching stories about personal loss, suicide, addiction, and divorce. These blogs painted such a realistic portrait that I felt that was already a close friend of the reader. I was shocked by how my mood darkened and my thoughts turned inward as I lived a through another person's writing.
>
> I've also read posts that took me to the summit of K2, hiking along the Appalachian Trail, into small country kitchens, and on the first date with a teen struck by puppy love. The authors allowed me to be "the fly on the wall" and opened up their private thoughts to my curious eye.

These bloggers are incredibly brave. They are also authentically human. All of them are doing exactly what they were wired to do—dream, tell stories, persuade, teach, curate, and share the things that are most precious to them.

It's fascinating to imagine a future when historians dig through archaic flash drives filled with blog entries. For the first time archaeologists will have the emotional history of our culture. Unlike cave wall art, stone carvings, or papyrus tablets, our civilization has a canvas that is infinite in size. Our sharing is only restricted by our time, insight and experience. It's thrilling to think that with blogging, no one has to fear being forgotten. If you're a blogger, you're leaving a permanent digital footprint.

Blogs would still be an extraordinary tool even if they were just a one-way public diary. Thankfully, blogging offers two-way commenting, giving readers the chance to publicly support or confront the writer.

Blog comments can be both uplifting and toxic. Go on to any large blog and you'll see the worst side of people. Many popular bloggers completely ignore their comments because they rarely see any thoughtful and relevant feedback. Add the constant onslaught of spambots that overwhelm blogs with advertisements for porn and illegal drugs, and it's no wonder bloggers are cautious about their comment section.

The benefits of real-time reader feedback, however, outweigh the challenges associated with commenting. Scanning through comments often yields priceless insights and perspectives. Bloggers have cultivated friendships, learned about new resources, expanded their networks, and even started new careers based on comments.

> **MARK:** I get about 25 percent of my ideas for new blog posts directly from the comment section. Several times a year a comment is so good, I ask the contributor if I can turn it into a stand-alone blog post!

Without comments, it's difficult to gauge if you are making emotional connections with your readers. Of course, you can argue that comments don't matter, but it's hard to buy that reasoning. The goal of "personal satisfaction" must have some sort of yardstick. If you are blogging purely for internal gratification, then a paper notebook would be all that's needed. However, when personal bloggers are pressed, they admit that they eagerly anticipate and read every comment. While comments may not influence their subject matter, they do inspire the blogger to stick with the process of "thinking in public."

The magic of personal blogging occurs when writers discover that the act of blogging is changing how they think and live. Katie Foster, the blogger behind *Runs for Cookies*, consciously decided to use a blog as an accountability partner. She knew that exposing her goals and weight-loss progress to the world would change the game. She couldn't hide without feeling guilty or publicly admitting that she had "quit."

Over time, the blog attracted friends and fellow weight-loss warriors who considered Katie to be a role model. "I felt that I couldn't let my audience down," Katie admits. "Having readers forced me to keep going." Tony Robbins calls the process of publicly committing to a goal "getting leverage over yourself."[1]

Katie's blog was perfect because thousands of monthly visitors waited to see how well she did during the month. Over time, achieving her weight-loss goals become routine. Her blog had been a valuable partner for keeping her on track.

Pat Flynn of *The Smart Passive Income Blog* (smartpassiveincome.com) gives his readers monthly reports of income earned from his growing empire of websites. Some are shocked that he's so open with information that most hold close to the vest. Like Katie, Pat sees the power in using his blog to push himself to excel. If he fails to hit his income goals, he has to explain why. These explanations are brutally honest. Pat grows from the experience and uses the setback to rethink and experiment with new tactics. The other benefit is that Pat's widely regarded as the most knowledgeable and authentic marketer in an otherwise "slippery" marketplace.

MARK: Although I regard my blog *{grow}* primarily as a business blog that establishes voice of authority in my market, I also show my personal side, and taking that risk has definitely helped me grow as a person.

The blog post that probably created the greatest reaction from my audience started like this: "I am feeling sad and a bit ashamed of myself." Not your usual lead for a business story, is it?

I went on to tell the story about my friendship with a woman named Jenn Whinnem. Jenn and I had collaborated on a few projects virtually, and we had had been Twitter buddies for more than two years. She had been a frequent commenter on my blog community, and I felt I had grown to know her.

I was dumbfounded when I read on another blog that she had a terminal disease, cystic fibrosis, and suffers every day. Until that moment, I had put Jenn in the category of "personal friend," but I realized I did not even know this single important fact that dominates her life, in fact dominates every breath she takes. I hadn't even talked to her on the phone. I would have heard the coughing. I would have asked her about it. I could have, and should have, known.

I lost sight of what it means to be a friend. It's a word that has been social-media cheapened and distorted for a new generation, and I got caught up in it too.

This revelation had a profound impact on me, and I decided to humbly and honestly discuss it on the blog. I realized that I was not getting to know the people behind the little avatars in my blog community and invited people to just call me so we could get to know each other. I wrote:

> *It's ironic that a thousand blog posts have been written about the importance of "the conversation but the social web actually helps us avoid conversations through status updates and other non-invasive procedures. I've decided that I want to do better. I want to have real conversations and make real friends. I have gained so much from actually*

> *talking on the phone—and even meeting—the people on {grow}. And yet, most of you are still strangers. Want to talk? Call me.*

> What followed was an amazing outpouring of connection from my blog community. 150 comments in all saying they were moved, understood, sympathized, and that yes, they were going to call. These conversations were the most important and rewarding benefit of my entire blogging career.

> And, as you might have expected, my first call was to Jenn.

Unlike a memoir that reflects back on a career, personal bloggers examine their life, emotions, and outcomes in the moment. It seems appropriate that the increasing speed of information technology has turned self-reflection into a high-speed, real-time activity. If blogging ensures you won't be forgotten, the merging of social networking, search technology, and blogging guarantees that you'll never have to face a challenge alone.

After considering the personal benefits of blogging, it's easy to argue that everyone should try it. It's easy to see the beneficial effects of social technology. Isn't it time that we individually accept the challenge of making ourselves better by sharing our personal journey with others?

Now, we'll shift our attention to helping you experience the benefits of personal blogging. We'll walk you through the questions you should consider and show you how to experience the full benefit of blogging for personal benefit.

Note

[1] http://www.tonyrobbins.com/leadership2012/The-Power-of -Leverage.pdf.

CHAPTER 19

Breaking Through with a Personal Blog

I f you're ready to try a personal blog, it makes sense to spend a little time planning.

Personal blogging should be approached with the same careful attention to detail as business blogging. Even 60 minutes spent thinking through your personal blogging strategy will deliver incredible results. Many bloggers later realize that their hobby blog is a viable business but discover that mistakes have made it harder for them to make the transition. Others start blogs that turn into a guilt-ridden chore that they end up hating.

In the end, your personal blog should make you feel happy, fulfilled, powerful, and connected to a larger community. Let's make sure that you experience those benefits.

Before you sign up for a blog profile or write your first post, write down what you believe the objective should be for your blog. This objective is your mission statement for the blog. It's focused on your needs and the results you want to receive.

OBJECTIVES OF PERSONAL BLOGS

Personal bloggers usually select one of the following three objectives: accountability, introspection, and sharing.

Accountability

Are you trying to get leverage on yourself by publicly declaring your goals? Do you want your audience to call you out if your willpower slips? Writing an accountability blog requires ruthless honesty and discipline. Accountability doesn't work if you hide your weaknesses.

Accountability blogs work incredibly well for people with easily quantifiable goals such as weight loss, learning a new skill, or breaking the grip of addiction.

The first post on your blog will likely be a contract with your readers. Your contract will tell them what you want, how you plan to get it, and the role you want them to play. Friends, family, and colleagues will be your first readers and perhaps your harshest critics. Accountability takes courage, and putting yourself out there for everyone to see is incredibly brave.

Introspection

Do you want to turn a magnifying glass on your thinking? Do you want a record of how your perspective changes over time? Introspective blogs act as breadcrumbs on your journey through life. They help you peel away the outer shell of your thoughts and dig down to the core reasons for your behavior, beliefs, and values.

Some of the best introspective blogs are nurtured by college students and "warrior survivors" of life-threatening diseases, accidents, or life circumstances. Every day is recorded and evaluated. Simply seeing your thoughts on the screen will give you the power to change how you respond to the world.

Outside readers may have a tough time with your posts unless you take a step back and tell them the story behind the blog. The people who stick with your blog will become ardent supporters who will dutifully comment on your daily musings and offer encouragement or a new viewpoint.

Introspective blogs are often temporary. Many times the blogger moves past the circumstance that inspired the blog. Don't feel bad about this. Tuck away your posts for a time in the future when you can revisit that period in your life. Heck, these posts might be the start of your memoirs.

Sharing

A sharing blog exists to share fascinating and specific information. The blog often has the same role as a scientist's lab notebook—every observation and test result is recorded. The blogger gets a special thrill in being the first to share his or her work, ideas, and opinions. Readers are often just as obsessed with the blog's subject as the publisher is. They actively comment to add to or poke holes in the information the blogger provides. Regardless, everyone is thrilled to participate in the pursuit of the next piece of wow info.

Sharing blogs are the classic hobbyist journals written by dedicated enthusiasts and cover every imaginable passion and interest. If you have an activity that you are fanatically obsessed with, then you have the foundation for a terrific sharing blog!

These blogs are relatively easy to write because you are simply sharing what you love. It is probably more difficult *not* to share your hobby discoveries. You'll have a voracious audience that will visit your blog regularly. These people are just as obsessed as you are and will be on the hunt for new information.

Sharing blogs that attract a sizable audience are relatively easy to convert into profitable business blogs. Your audience is used to investing in their hobby. If your blog offers excellent product advice, it's very likely that you will find an audience that is ready to buy.

YOUR BLOG'S STYLE

Now that we've reviewed the basic types of blog you can start, it's time to think about your blogging style.

Like business blogging, your style will be dependent on the core blogging skills you naturally lean toward. Since you already have a core blogging skill preference (see Chapter 9), all you have to do is identify it and begin using it in your blog posts.

Let's review each skill through the lens of personal blogging:

- **Dreamers.** Dreamers focus on the world as it could be. Their blog is a vehicle to describing their vision and influencing others to get on board. Dreamers feel comfortable with introspective blogs that allow them to experiment with new thoughts and perspectives.
- **Storytellers.** Storytellers see themselves as a character in an evolving drama. Storytellers use accountability blogs and introspective blogs to recruit new characters and uncover new experiences.
- **Persuaders.** Persuaders have a clear point of view and put the world into three groups: supporters, fence-sitters, and enemies. They often display the dreamer skill as well since their ideals are firmly anchored in a vision of the world as it should be. Persuaders use their blog to debate, mobilize their supporters, and recruit new soldiers for the cause.
- **Teachers.** Teachers are most comfortable when they are simplifying the complex. They see themselves as

lifelong students and are intensely curious about the world around them. Teachers often are natural storytellers as well, intuitively understanding that stories are powerful teaching tools. Teachers understand the effectiveness of all three personal blogging types but tend to favor introspective and sharing blogs.

- **Curators.** Curators collect, organize, and display. Their blog is a canvas or stage for the collections they've painstakingly assembled. Curators often let their work speak for itself. Text gets in the way, yielding to photos and video. Curators are often passionate hobbyists with a deep knowledge on a specific subject, prompting them to use the sharing blog type.

Using these descriptions can help you pinpoint where you fit. As we've mentioned before, it's common for people to manifest two or three of the core blogging skills. One skill, however, will feel more comfortable and will be your dominant skill. Start here and use the skill descriptions to help you make wise decisions about your blog topics and writing voice.

PERFECT IS THE ENEMY OF GOOD

Easy does it. Right now, look for the path that will get you up and blogging as quickly as possible. It's easy to complicate an easy task with distractions. You don't have to have perfect graphics. You don't have to become an expert at CSS or HTML coding. You don't have to memorize Strunk and White's *Elements of Style* and hone your grammar skills to a fine edge.

All you need to do is write. Don't polish the cannonball, as they say. You would be amazed at how popular simple blogs can be.

Let's walk through some straightforward basic requirements so you can get up and going on your blog right away.

PICKING THE BEST BLOGGING PLATFORM

WordPress, Tumblr, and Blogspot are the top options for building and managing blogs. Each has its own strengths and weaknesses, which are outlined in this section.

WordPress

WordPress offers two options: a self-hosted option where you download the software and upload it to your own server and a hosted option where WordPress hosts your blog for you. We'll describe the pros and cons of the hosted solution.

Pros
- **Free:** You can set up your blog and launch it free. You can upgrade to paid versions to get more publishing and customization as your budget allows.
- **Easy:** No technical skills are needed to set up your blog. The entire process is menu driven. Select your name, choose a template design, and start writing your first blog post.
- **Good template options:** WordPress.com offers 218 blog templates to choose from. Each of these templates can be customized slightly to match your tastes. More are being added frequently.

Cons
- **Limited flexibility:** You will need to stick with the options offered by WordPress. Customizations are limited to what the service offers.

- **Creative restrictions:** Users are restricted to the existing template choices for the look and feel of the blog. You can make slight tweaks to the template options, but you won't be able to make extensive changes without paying for an upgrade.
- **Domain/branding:** Free users must use a web address that includes wordpress.com such as your-domain.wordpress.com. These WordPress-branded domains could confuse blog visitors and detract from your branding. You can upgrade your membership to get a custom domain; however, this could stretch the budget of someone looking for a low- or no-cost blogging solution.

Tumblr

Tumblr is described as a microblogging service that supports short blog posts called asides, photo posting, and link sharing—essentially Twitter on steroids.

Pros
- **Free:** You can keep your wallet in your pocket. All you need is a username, e-mail, and password, and you are all set.
- **Easy setup:** Tumblr will start you off with an attractive template that you can start filling with content immediately. Every menu is pared down to the absolute minimum. It will even fill your blog with content selected from other Tumblr users.
- **Customizable:** Tumblr will let you customize every element of your blog. You can use the drop-down menus or tinker with the CSS to achieve a specific look.

Cons

- **Tough for writers:** Tumblr's options are geared for artists, photographers, and graphic designers. Text-focused posts look basic on the platform, possibly hurting readability.
- **Tumblr branding:** Like WordPress.com, your brand will be connected to the Tumblr brand (yourdomain. tumblr.com). The good news is that Tumblr won't charge you to use a custom domain.
- **Learning curve:** Although setup and posting are point-and-click easy, advanced features take a while to understand. Tumblr's willingness to give you full control of every element of your blog actually makes it more complicated for the simple user.

Blogger/Blogspot

Blogger was the first hosted blogging service to go mainstream. The service distinguished itself by being easy to use and free. Google purchased Blogger in 2003, exponentially growing its user base and making it the de facto blogging platform for millions of bloggers.

Pros

- **Free:** Blogger pioneered the concept of free-for-all blogging. Google extended the free perks, offering no-cost domain hosting and 1 gigabyte of free photo hosting.
- **Integrated with Google:** Blogger is tightly integrated with Google's other services like Google Analytics for web tracking statistics. Users can also access their blog via the ubiquitous toolbar within Gmail, Google. com, and Google+.

- **Easy:** Setting up a Blogspot blog is simple and intuitive. Basic blog features are easily customized through a point-and-click interface.

Cons

- **Basic templates:** The standard templates are extremely basic with limited customization options.
- **Minimal SEO customization:** Surprisingly, there are few search engine optimization features such as tagging and easy customization of meta information.
- **Difficult customization:** Template changes require knowledge of HTML and CSS. The customization interface is minimal and offers few options for changing template elements.

Where to Host Your Blog

Overall we recommend WordPress's hosted option if you need a low-maintenance, easy-to-set-up platform. You'll sacrifice flexibility and customization, but WordPress's advantages still offer an attractive and professional starting point.

If you are comfortable with hosting and installing software, then use the self-hosted version of WordPress available at wordpress.org. This will give you all the flexibility you need as your blog grows.

Tumblr and Blogspot come with prebuilt creative themes that can easily be customized to your taste. Again, don't kill yourself over these details. It's likely that you will change your blog design dozens of times in the next few years. Select a design that you won't mind staring at for six months and go to the next step.

One caveat: If you plan to use photos extensively on your blog, look for a design specifically created for photos. Often these creative templates will be designed for photo galleries and showrooms.

BLOG SETUP CHECKLIST

Once you've set up your hosting and configured your software, you are ready to optimize your blog for success. Here's a list to make sure you have all of your bases covered:

- **Blog name**. Your blog's name will be the first thing your reader sees. Select a name that communicates your blog's goal. Feel free to be clever, but not so clever that you confuse your reader.
- **Tagline.** Taglines are usually a sentence appearing directly below your blog title. Use your tagline to promise your reader a benefit. Adam Baker's tagline for his blog *Man vs. Debt* is "Sell your crap. Pay off your debt. Do what you love." *Man vs. Debt* readers understand exactly what they are getting. How about your readers?
- **Overall look and feel.** Your blog revolves around your blog text. Make sure that nothing distracts from the content you'll be posting. Think carefully before you clutter your design with advertising, busy graphics, and animation.
- **The actual blog post.** Readers will scan your blog looking for post headlines. Help them get to the right place by making your headlines bold and easy to read.
- **Select a font that is easy to read at any size.** The traditional fonts like Times New Roman, Arial, and Verdana work in almost any situation. Avoid script and handwriting type fonts that are extremely difficult to read at a glance.

- **Photos.** Check how photos appear in your blog posts. Photos liven up your posts and add character to your blog. Make sure you can easily add photos with minimum fuss.
- **Commenting.** WordPress and other blogging platforms have commenting systems built into the software. However, third-party software developers have created add-ons to expand the basic capability of the standard comment systems. Popular choices include Disqus, Livefyre, and IntenseDebate. Each add-on offers reliable commenting while adding social sharing features and options for encouraging readers to return to the blog to check on new comment submissions. Review each of the options and select the one that fits the objectives of your blog.
- **Sidebars.** Be selective about the items you put in your sidebar. Often sidebars are choked with miles of plug-ins, widgets, ads, and other stuff. The more stuff you pack in, the less likely that your reader will pay attention to any of it. Your sidebar should offer readers options for building a relationship with you, joining your community, and exploring more blog content. We recommend starting with a form for offering blog updates by e-mail, showing recent posts, a bio with your photo, and an invitation to join your audience on two or three of your favorite social platforms.
- **Footer.** Use your footer to display copyright information, disclosures, and legalese. Although your footer isn't prominent, resist the urge to clutter it up with everything that didn't make it into your sidebar.

You should be off to a great start! Your blog will work hard for you if you cover the bases using the information we've provided. The challenge now is to establish habits that will help you consistently publish the best content possible. We'll focus on those habits next.

CHAPTER 20

Blogging Habits

B logging success is built on mastering your specific combination of skills and traits. Like anything, the best results come from turning key activities into habits.

Close examination of successful personal blogs point to four important habits. The following sections explore how you can put those habits into practice.

HABIT 1: WRITE EVERY DAY— PUBLISH ON A SCHEDULE

We can learn a lesson from the great science fiction writer Isaac Asimov. People marveled at his consistency and his voluminous creative output. His strategy was simple: write 1,000 words every day. Now that doesn't sound like a lot. In analog terms, that's roughly two pages of double-spaced type. But add it up. He could write the equivalent of one paperback science fiction book every month—12 books a year, just by adhering to that discipline.

The best bloggers commit to putting words on "paper" every day. Some write in the morning, others late in the evening. Regardless of their preference, these bloggers make a point of writing a specific number of words per day. The word count goal is arbitrary. You can select 100 words or 1,000 words. The point is to get your brain used to organizing thoughts and expressing them on paper.

Writing is different from publicly publishing your post. While you might publish a post twice a week, you should still write every day. Once you've established a daily writing habit, your library of post ideas will increase as you tinker with new ideas during your writing period.

> **STANFORD:** I learned early on that the best way to get comfortable with writing was too write a lot. Surprisingly, I always had something to write about. It seemed that my brain just needed a set time to unload its daily observations.
>
> I began carrying a little notebook with me to capture idea snippets. At night, around 9 p.m., I would fetch the notebook and write 100 words on any of the ideas. Many times these "writing sketches" turned into full posts. I've never been at a loss for post ideas once I established this writing habit.

> **MARK:** I have an unpredictable schedule that revolves around teaching and consulting, so I can't have a set daily writing schedule. Instead I block out Sunday mornings before I go to church as my sacred blogging time. I get up before anybody else, put on a pot of coffee, and write for three or four hours. In that time, I can create at least two solid blog posts for the week. Like Stanford, I constantly collect ideas so that when it's time to get going, I don't have to waste time thinking up an idea. I just pluck out my favorite snippet and get right to it.

> **TAKE ACTION**
>
> It's said that time is the great equalizer. We all have the same amount of time every day. You have the same amount of time today as Joyce Carol Oates, who wrote 100 books in 45 years. The difference is how you prioritize your time. You make time for priorities. Commit today to dedicate 15 minutes to writing every day—starting now.

HABIT 2: MASTER YOUR SUBJECT

Commit to mastering your specific natural skill. If you are a teacher, then research and implement different teaching styles in your writing. Curators should look for examples of renowned researchers, art curators, and collectors for ideas on compiling and categorization.

Look beneath the surface topics and dig deep into the supporting evidence for your subject. These details will add relevance and power to your blogging. Readers will flock to your blog knowing that you offer a fresh and in-depth perspective.

STANFORD: I write about blogging. Many believed at first that I picked the wrong subject, but thankfully, they were wrong. I routinely find new material, historical perspective, and stories about blogging that many overlook. Ironically, my understanding of blogging accelerated when I ignored other "blogging blogs." I took my own direction looking for blogging advice in screenplay writing, myths and legends, anthropology, American Revolutionary literature, and even quantum physics!

MARK: Everyone hits writer's block now and then. If you simply don't have a great idea one week, comment on somebody else's. As you immerse yourself in your passion, you are probably constantly reading about the amazing things you love. When you come across an outstanding article, write a blog commentary about the article. Talk about what you like and what you disagree with. Be sure to give proper credit to the original author with a link back to the original work. He or she will appreciate the nod and the effort you put into continuing the conversation.

TAKE ACTION

Approach your subject as if you were learning it for the first time. Start with a Wikipedia search and read the information with fresh eyes. Review the article citations, read supporting books, and do research on key contributors to your field.

If your blog focuses on your daily experiences, then view yourself as a research subject! Research your family tree to understand the history surrounding you and your family. Unearth the motivations and aspirations behind your habits, choice of friends, and career. You are much more interesting than you realize.

Set aside time to dive down the "rabbit hole" and spend an extended amount of time researching and thinking about your subject. Look for the stories and unique facts that get overlooked by others.

HABIT 3: IGNITE CONVERSATION

Blogging is a social medium. It works best when you can talk with your readers and draw from their experiences. But according to Internet think tank Forrester, just 37 percent of readers want to leave a comment.[1]

Readers fear negative reactions from you and other readers. Your job is to lower their resistance to commenting by demonstrating your willingness to engage with every reader.

The secret to commenting is to write posts that are conversational and approachable. Directly addressing the reader throughout your posts and asking open-ended questions prompts the reader to respond in the comments section.

Imagine that your readers are sitting in front of you and you are walking them through your thoughts. We naturally pause for feedback in conversations. Work the same pauses into your post. It's OK to ask, "Does this make sense?" as you write. Your readers will mentally answer your question and be primed to respond when they get to the comments section.

People who write large blogs, which depend heavily on reader reactions, have learned that emotionally charged topics prompt a response. The emotion can be positive or negative as long as it's a strong response. The same applies to your personal blog. Show people the emotional power behind your words. You might do this already. If not, concentrate on revealing emotion in concrete ways. Practice this in your daily writing. Over time, your candid expression of passion and energy will work its way into your writing, giving it force and relevance.

MARK: It was such a surprise and delight when people started commenting on my blog! I was blown away that people would actually take their time to read my writing and leave a comment. Isn't that a wonderful gift?

That's the way I approach a comment from my community—it's a gift. I figure the least I can do is respond back, and I do. Yes, this can be time-consuming. Sometimes I respond to blog comments at one in the morning, but I always do it. I want my community to feel appreciated.

I also go out of my way to make people feel welcome, even when they dissent. I try to knock down barriers and let people know it's a safe place for discussion. I think that has helped grow the community a lot.

Fear of haters coming onto a blog makes some people intimidated about blogging. As of the time I am writing this book, I have had 25,000 comments on my blog, and here is how many I have deleted: 5. That's two hundredths of a percent. That doesn't mean I *liked* them all, but the comments were at least fair. Don't stop yourself from blogging out of fear of negative comments.

TAKE ACTION

Before you start writing, identify two or three questions that could spark conversation. The questions could touch on a popular discussion in your niche or prompt your readers to share their reactions to your post. Don't be afraid of constructive criticism or prompting a strong reaction. Healthy and respectful discussion is good for your community.

HABIT 4: BUILDING YOUR SUPPORT TEAM

Blogging is lonely. It's just you huddled over a keyboard tapping out your inner thoughts. In the beginning, you might publish dozens of posts before you receive a comment. There will be few retweets or Facebook likes. You will feel that no one is listening or even cares.

Plan for the lonely times from the beginning. Look for opportunities to talk with other people in the "real world" about your blog and the process of writing. Take the first step and join online discussion forums focused on your subject. Comment on complementary blogs offering encouragement and new perspectives.

As new readers join your blogging community, do all that you can to celebrate their contributions and support. Visit their blogs and comment when appropriate. E-mail or call loyal readers and offer your support and guidance. Invite like-minded bloggers to submit a guest post for publication on your blog. These people are your new friends, so do all that you can to build the relationship.

> **STANFORD:** I was blessed to have commenters within two months. One of my blog posts did extremely well and brought in lots of new readers. I worked hard to answer comments and e-mail people who had interesting viewpoints. I also participated in several Twitter chats.
>
> During the Twitter chats, dozens of people followed me on Twitter and quite a few visited my blog and commented on posts. These chats offered me an invaluable forum to test out ideas and get feedback while my blog was new.
>
> **MARK:** I agree with Stanford, but personally, I hate Twitter chats. I have a hard time following any meaningful conversation when the tweets are flying so fast. Here are three other places I found support during the lonely start-up period:
>
> 1. LinkedIn forums. There are many groups dedicated to social media and blogging, and the people in these discussion groups will spend so much time helping you!
> 2. Blogger buddies. Find three or four other bloggers who are also just starting out. Support each other by commenting and promoting one another's blog posts. Even today I have

a Google hangout once a month with a few friendly fellow bloggers.

3. Meet live with other bloggers in your hometown. Many cities have a social media club of some kind, and even small towns have dedicated bloggers of some kind. It doesn't matter what people are blogging about. The issues we face are pretty much universal.

TAKE ACTION

In our busy world, it's sometimes hard to take the time to think, let alone network and get support. But the early months of blogging can be very lonely and even depressing. Whether it's a Twitter chat, a LinkedIn group, or the local social media club, seek out fellow bloggers to help you through the tough spots and offer the encouragement you need to stick with it.

Note

[1]http://blogs.forrester.com/jackie_rousseau_anderson/10-09-28 -latest_global_social_media_trends_may_surprise_you.

CHAPTER 21

Coda

Whether blogging for business, for money, or for personal enjoyment, the experience can be an emotional roller coaster!

You're bound to hit some rough patches and self-doubt. And when you do, we'd like you to remember this final story:

Dr. Alice Ackerman is a pediatrician and college educator from Virginia Tech University who started blogging after being inspired by the book *The Tao of Twitter*.

She put a lot of thought into her blog and decided that this would be an excellent vehicle for community outreach. Specifically, one of the goals would be educate her rural community about the importance of childhood inoculation, a subject with a lot of misunderstandings surrounding it.

Since she was part of both a hospital and a university, it was a real struggle to get approval for a blog in any form, but she persevered and eventually got the go-ahead. However, finding an audience for her blog posts turned out to be even more difficult.

Despite her efforts to provide interesting, helpful posts on a consistent basis, she had some doubt as to whether she was making an impact. She kept a Google Analytics chart displaying the lowly results of her blogging efforts. For more than a year, her posts limped along, averaging 4.5 readers a day.

And then something magical happened. She received this tweet:

Dr. Ackerman is the person who changed my mind about vaccinations once I read her blog and her links. I had no idea that information existed.

Through this simple message, Dr. Ackerman realized that her work had indeed been worthwhile. "Yes, I only had 4.5 readers a day on my blog," she said, "but I had an impact on one of them. Thank goodness I never stopped." And shortly after this event, her blog began to pick up steam.

This is a profound lesson for all of us:

- "Citizen Influencers" like Dr. Ackerman are using the power of online publishing tools to make a difference in unexpected ways.
- You may never really know when your words are making an impact.
- Tenacity, commitment, patience, and the courage to keep going make the difference in blogging success.

You have this power to make a difference, too. Now that we can have access to the high-speed Internet and free blogging tools, your voice can be heard. Don't waste this opportunity!

We'd like to end the book with a quote that Mark uses on the last slide of the last class he teaches to his students. It's a comment that was left on his blog by a student many years ago:

Social media marketing is not something that can be taught—it has to be experienced, and this is why schools have a hard time teaching classes about it. Students who take advantage of social media will have a leg up on those who do not. Formal education and books can show you the

*tools . . . but it is up to YOU to learn how to apply them for
you and your business.*

We are grateful that you've read our book. But no matter
how many times you return to it, you can't master blogging
until you immerse yourself in the platform and learn by
doing. So we want to encourage you to be persistent, patient,
present, and above all, courageous with your blogging.

Now what are you waiting for? Write.

Index

About the Authors

Mark W. Schaefer is a globally recognized blogger, speaker, educator, business consultant, and author who blogs at {grow}—one of the top marketing blogs of the world. Mark has worked in global sales, PR, and marketing positions for nearly 30 years and now provides consulting services as executive director of U.S.-based Schaefer Marketing Solutions.

Mark has advanced degrees in marketing and organizational development and holds seven patents. He is a faculty member of the graduate studies program at Rutgers University and is the founder of Social Slam, a national social media event that takes place each April. He is the author of two bestselling marketing books, *Return on Influence* and *The Tao of Twitter*. In 2012, he was named by *Forbes* magazine as one of the Top 50 social media "power influencers" of the world.

Mark has appeared on many national television shows and in periodicals including the *Wall Street Journal*, *Wired*, the *New York Times*, and the CBS News. Follow his blog at www.businessesgrow.com and on Twitter: @markwschaefer.

Stanford Smith is the managing director at Pushing Social, a social media and content marketing consultancy. Stanford has over 15 year of experience crafting award-winning digital marketing campaigns and social media programs for Fortune 500 brands, state organizations, and start-ups. Social Media Examiner has recognized the *Pushing Social* blog as one of the Top 10 social media blogs in the world.

Stanford is a well-known guest contributor to a "who's who" list of top social media blogs including *Copyblogger*, *Problogger*, *Write to Done*, *Convince and Convert*, and {grow}. You can see his latest work at pushingsocial.com and follow him on Twitter at twitter.com/pushingsocial.